Setting and Streaming

A RESEARCH REVIEW

Wynne Harlen
and
Heather Malcolm

The Scottish Council for Research in Education

SCRE Publication 143
Using Research Series 18 (*formerly* Practitioner Minipaper Series)

Series editors: Valerie Wilson
                  Rosemary Wake

First published 1997

Revised edition 1999

ISBN 1 86003 049 1

Cover photograph: Simon Saffery
Grateful thanks to pupils at Gracemount Primary School, Edinburgh

Design and typesetting by SCRE Information Services.

Printed and bound in Great Britain for the Scottish Council for Research in Education, 15 St John Street, Edinburgh EH8 8JR, by Bell & Bain, 303 Burnfield Road, Thornliebank, Glasgow G46 7UQ.

Contents

1
Introduction

The first edition of this review was written at the request of the Scottish Office Education and Industry Department (SOEID) to inform an inquiry into the organisation and management of classes in primary and secondary schools. The terms of reference specified 'a critical review of the literature pertaining to the ability grouping of classes and within classes. Particular attention should be directed at the literature on tracking in the USA'. A tight time-scale was set for the completion of the review so that it could feed into the work of the SOEID group (which later published its recommendations in *Achievement for All* (SOEID, 1996).

Interest in ability grouping has become greater and more widespread since the publication of the SOEID report and of Department for Education and Employment (DfEE) documents giving official encouragement for the practice of setting. It is easy for the debate to be swayed by anecdotes and media headlines, since, as in many aspects of education, values dictate the interpretation of evidence. Whilst it is important to hear different opinions and debate the arguments for and against policies on setting and mixed-ability grouping, it is essential to know what has been found from systematic study of actual practice. Therefore, to keep abreast of developments in the research we have updated this review to include more recent studies and others that were missed in our earlier trawl.

As before, the two reviews by Slavin (1987 and 1990) form an important point of entry into the research. However, we are indebted to Slavin not only for the reviews of the earlier research but also for the methodology. The concept of 'best evidence synthesis' is one that Slavin borrowed from the profession of law and applied in reviewing research. It requires a reviewer to identify criteria for what is good quality research, yielding best evidence in a particular field. Having done this, the reviewer places more emphasis on the findings of those studies which match the criteria than on those which have some shortcomings. This does not mean that the latter are completely ignored, for there may be few studies which meet the criteria, but rather that 'we might cautiously examine the less well designed studies to see if there is adequate unbiased information to come to any conclusion' (Slavin, 1986). However, a 'health warning' is given in using the results.

The adherence to the strict use of criteria for best evidence is not always possible in cases where the reporting of research may lack the detail necessary to judge the extent of match. Thus we have sometimes found it difficult to reconcile contradictory findings. However, in our conclusions we have attempted to reflect the most consistent patterns without over-simplifying what will always be a complex issue influenced by a multitude of variables.

Organisation of the review

The review is straightforward in structure. After an initial section on definitions and some words of warning about the research methodology employed in studies in this area, the research is reviewed in two sections, dealing first with primary/elementary schools and then with secondary schools. In Chapter 2 the studies are grouped according to their focus on streaming, setting or within-class ability grouping. Chapter 3 has a somewhat different structure reflecting the greater amount of research that compares streaming and setting with mixed-ability teaching. Some attempt is made to consider differences according to the subject taught, but it has not been possible to review this systematically since the research is very unevenly spread across subjects, most dealing with reading and mathematics. The final chapter offers some conclusions which arise from the review. There is no attempt made to make recommendations, since any action in specific cases would depend on more than the grouping of pupils.

Definitions

Much of the research into setting and streaming has been conducted in schools in the US, where different terms from those in common use in the United Kingdom are used for various ways of organising schools and classrooms. At times the American research also covers organisational formats that have no exact British equivalent, such as the Joplin Plan. In this review, except when the context requires original wording, the British terms for groupings have been used. The definitions adopted are given in Figure 1 together with North American equivalents. The definitions of streaming, setting and banding used here are taken from the glossary to the HMI report *Aspects of Secondary Education in England* (DES, 1979).

Figure 1: Definition of British and American Terms

UK term	UK meaning	US equivalent
Streaming	The method of assigning pupils to classes on some overall assessment of general ability, the most able pupils in one stream, the next most able in the next and so on. The classes so streamed are used as the teaching units for the majority of subjects.	*Tracking/ Ability class assignment*
Setting	The regrouping of pupils according to their ability in the subject concerned. This can be carried out across the whole year group or within a band or population provided that two or more classes can be timetabled for the same subject at the same time. Setting can therefore be used within any pattern or organisation. Schools frequently seek to make teaching groups smaller and more homogeneous by providing extra sets; for example, by regrouping the 90 pupils in three classes into four or five sets, though staffing constraints make it unlikely that this can be done in more than a few subjects.	*Regrouping/ Curriculum assignment/ Departmentalization/ Joplin Plan (a special form for reading, which cuts across age groups)*
Banding	The year group is divided into two, three or four bands differentiated by ability on criteria similar to those used for streaming; each band contains a number of classes, not necessarily of equal ability or size.	*No US equivalent*
Mixed-ability grouping	No attempt is made to group pupils by ability. Instead year grouping may be done randomly or a deliberate mix may be achieved on the basis of factors such as social background or gender.	*Heterogeneous grouping*
Within-class grouping	Groups are formed by a teacher within a class to reduce the number of pupils receiving direct tuition at any one time. The groups may be homogeneous, organised on the basis of ability (usually in reading, although other criteria may be used), or mixed ability (heterogeneous).	*Within-class grouping*

The methodology of the review

In this review an attempt has been made to follow the approach of Best-Evidence Synthesis, as set out by Slavin (1986). In essence this sets out the criteria for the inclusion of studies in the review, systematically searches the literature for all studies meeting these criteria, describes them in sufficient depth for their essential features and findings to be communicated and brings together the results, where possible using meta-analyses (Glass *et al*, 1981). We have relied heavily on two comprehensive reviews carried out by Slavin, (1987, 1990) and one by Lou *et al* (1996) and have used the findings of their meta-analyses rather than carrying out our own. The research synthesis by Gamoran and Berends (1987) has also been a useful source. We have added to the studies reviewed by Slavin ones which have been carried out since his reviews and ones which have incorporated qualitative findings.

The criteria for inclusion of studies in the review are as follows:

- studies are of the effects of various forms of grouping by ability within schools and classes, not of the effects of allocation between schools

- studies concern primary and lower secondary school; reference is made to those involving older pupils only where the findings illuminate issues that apply generally for other age groups

- studies compare the experience and/or performance of pupils grouped by ability with those in mixed-ability groups or classes

- valid comparisons can be made; that is, in situations where pupils have either been allocated to groups randomly or where those within the groups compared are matched in terms of relevant variables such as initial ability and social background

- appropriate and reliable methods are used in making these comparisons

- differences between groups have existed for at least six months and preferably longer

- there is relevance to current debates either because of being conducted recently or having enduring significance.

Those studies which have been considered in depth are starred in the list of references. These include certain studies which were not taken into account because on closer examination they did not meet the criteria. At the same time not all studies meeting the criteria lead to useful findings. Thus before presenting the substance of the review there are some issues concerning the methods adopted within them which need to be aired.

Criticism of the research methods used

All studies reviewed, both quantitative and qualitative, suffer to some degree from the confounding of different effects inherent in the major question they address, which is 'how does grouping by ability affect learning?' In practice pupils are not put into groups or classes by ability and then treated in exactly the same way as if they were in mixed-ability groups or classes. Some would argue that this would be pointless, whilst others point to evidence that it is impossible since the different social mix and the value position of the teacher would inevitably change the class or group interactions. In other words it is never just the effect of grouping that is being compared but also the impact of different teaching methods, the quality of teaching, teacher expectations, pupil expectations and sometimes different materials. The effect of these associated factors varies with the age of the pupils, their gender, personalities and abilities (Webb, 1982).

In discussing heterogeneous and homogeneous grouping, Good and Marshall identify some difficulties that 'prevent a simple summary of the literature' (Good and Marshall, 1984, p16). They point out that homogeneous and heterogeneous are relative terms, depending on the school catchment area: 'We suspect that in some studies classes that were labelled heterogeneous were in fact more homogeneous than classes labelled as homogeneous in other studies.' Other variables, such as class size, can mediate the effect of homogeneity or heterogeneity, since a large homogeneous class may present the teacher with difficulties as great as in a small heterogeneous class. They also find that in some studies the treatment variable (content and methods) is kept, at least superficially, the same, but is modified in others, either to enrich the learning activities for the more able or to simplify and make less challenging those for the least able. Finally they claim that the teacher variable is central but cannot be separated from the composition variable. The evidence that these authors present in relation to the last of these is summarised in the next section.

To this list may be added, in the case of quantitative studies, the relevance of the measure used. Where there is a difference in the content or methods of the groups being compared, it is clearly important that the measure should reflect the learning experiences of both equally. Often this is impossible to judge since the same studies that depend on measures of achievement do not in general present detailed information about the teaching material and methods. Observational studies are needed for this. The gender bias in certain forms of assessment should also be kept in mind.

The difference in treatment of groups based on different ability and mixed-ability groups is a complex issue and threads throughout the literature. As we have suggested, there is little point in forming pupil groups by ability and then treating them in the same way as if they were of mixed ability, since the rationale for ability grouping is that it eases the provision of experiences appropriate to the pupils' ability. Yet if they are then given different treatment it is the effect of the treatment as much as of the grouping that is being measured. The point is made particularly well by reference to an extreme case, reported by Slavin (1990). In a US study, Mikkelson (1962) randomly assigned high-achieving lower secondary pupils to homogeneous or heterogeneous mathematics groups. Some pupils in the high ability groups were given enrichment whilst others were accelerated to the work of the next grade in algebra. Only those accelerated showed any difference from the mixed-ability groups. The conclusion that Slavin draws is that the research that compares different grouping within the same courses should not be taken as indicating the effects that are possible when ability grouping is used to provide different courses and challenges. In such cases it is clearly the difference in the course and the teaching that is having the effect. In theory the differentiated learning opportunities could be provided in a mixed-ability context.

It is also suggested by several studies, however, that attempts to control the 'treatment' of ability groups and mixed-ability groups being compared, and thus to get closer to measuring the effect of grouping *per se*, are doomed by the teacher variable. Gregory (1984) points out that in the research by Barker-Lunn (1970), often regarded as a model study in this area, there was a difference in the numbers of teachers who were favourably and unfavourably disposed to mixed-ability teaching, with more of the latter. It is not unreasonable to suppose that those with a negative attitude towards mixed-ability will be less willing or able to adopt teaching methods appropriate to this form of grouping. Again, without classroom observation it is impossible to be sure of this.

We have come across two studies that attempted to control the teacher effect by using the same teacher to teach the pupils first in ability groups and then in mixed-ability groups. Wallen and Vowles (1960) reported a small positive effect of within-class ability grouping for mathematics with a sixth grade class (11 year-olds). They were taught for one term in ability groups and then for one term as a whole mixed-ability class. Higher first term scores for the ability-grouped pupils were almost neutralised in the second term. Plewes (1979) regrouped the first year of a secondary school intake for science lessons half-way through the year. Some were in four mixed-ability teaching groups and some in four teaching groups setted by ability, based on IQ. After the half-year test the groups were interchanged. Apart from the disruption to the pupils, Plewes admitted that the process involved 'split personalities' for the teachers, 'but all entered into the spirit of the experiment'. The teaching methods were quite different in the two sets, with the mixed-ability groups being taught by individualised instruction methods. Thus the confounding of variables is such that it is hardly possible to give the results any credence, quite apart from the small number of pupils (61, probably because the school was an Army school with a high pupil turnover) for whom complete results were collected.

Finally, the vast majority of studies lack information of the kind that would enable conclusions to be drawn about how or why the composition of groups does or does not make a difference. Such information could come from classroom observations and from interviews with pupils and teachers. Studies using qualitative or ethnographic data have mainly concerned either young pupils learning to read (see Chapter 2) or older secondary pupils studying particular subjects (see the work of Boaler, reviewed on p45).

Gamoran and Berends (1987) have discussed the relative merits of ethnographic and survey research in the context of reviewing studies of the effects of streaming. They found more consistency among the ethnographic findings than among the findings from surveys. However, ethnographic studies give no indication of the magnitudes of any differences found, nor of their causal role in relation to achievement. Nevertheless qualitative studies show 'clear and consistent between-track differences ... and these differences may be linked to outcomes for students' (p430). This is not difficult to accept when the consistently reported differences are in the pace of instruction, the way tasks are organised and the frequent assignment of the more experienced and successful teachers to high-level streams.

Surveys which rely on outcome measures only, suffer from the methodological difficulties mentioned here and often provide inconsistent results. These short-comings suggest that it would be unwise to base policy-decisions on quantitative data alone. Not surprisingly, Gamoran and Berends call for a combination of ethnographic and survey research so that the differences observed by the former can be studied quantitatively and over time by the latter. At the same time, further ethnographic work is needed 'for a more theoretically grounded view of instruction' (p432).

2

Primary School Level

Streaming

Streaming was the norm in primary schools large enough to make it possible, as it was also in secondary schools, until the late 1960s. Jackson's (1964) survey of junior schools in England and Wales found that 96% of schools large enough for streaming were adopting this form of organisation. His survey found that the vast majority of headteachers were in favour of streaming despite the shortcomings that his work identified. Among these shortcomings were the prevalence of the lower streams being taught by less qualified teachers and being under-challenged. These findings are thought to have been among those influencing the Plowden Committee (CACE, 1967) to recommend the abolition of streaming in primary schools (page 291).

As further studies (eg Hargreaves, 1967; Lacey, 1970) into streaming in the secondary schools revealed negative effects, streaming in the primary school began to lose favour and quite rapidly disappeared during the 1970s and 1980s. Goldstein and Noss (1990) suggest that this was not a result of policy backed by evidence but that:

> To a large extent, the commitment to mixed ability teaching came from below, as a response on the part of classroom teachers to the expectations raised by the introduction of comprehensive schooling in the fifties and sixties. Some of the best practice was and is in primary schools, where the number of pupils in any given year renders it unviable to have more than a single class. Significantly, the abolition of the 11-plus and the accompanying removal of the need to assess pupils competitively gave a boost to this process.

> (Goldstein and Noss, 1990, p5)

Research comparing the achievements of pupils in streamed and unstreamed classes in general gives little support for the view that streaming increases achievement. Most of this research was carried out outside the UK for the reason that, when streaming was popular, there were few unstreamed schools for comparison, and, as Goldstein and Noss noted, the move to unstreaming did not depend on research evidence. The main exception to this was the study carried out in England by Barker-Lunn (1970). This featured in the comprehensive review of pre-1985 research into the effects of ability grouping carried out by Slavin (1987).

Studies of pupil achievement

Slavin's meticulous use of the 'best-evidence' technique described in Chapter 1 gives his findings considerable weight. Slavin's criteria were that in all the studies included:

- ability-grouped classes were compared to heterogeneously grouped control classes
- achievement data from standardised tests were presented
- the initial comparability of samples was established by use of random assignment, matching of classes, or matching of pupils within equivalent classes
- ability grouping was in place for at least a semester
- at least three experimental and three control teachers were involved.

These criteria excluded studies based only on observation or on teachers' or pupils' attitudes towards ability grouping. Evidence of this kind was sought from other studies for the present review.

Overall, Slavin found that there are no effects of streaming on pupils' achievements. Findings were mixed, some providing evidence that low achievers suffer (Borg, 1965; Flair, 1964; Tobin, 1966); others the opposite (Bremer, 1958; Hartill, 1936; Morgenstern, 1963) while others found no difference (Barker-Lunn, 1970; Goldberg, Passow and Justman, 1966; Loomer, 1962 and Rankin, Anderson and Bergman, 1936). One study (Cartwright and McIntosh, 1972) showed mixed-ability classes to do better in reading and mathematics, but Slavin cautions that the study has important limitations; in other words that evidence from this source would be discounted in comparison with better quality evidence.

Slavin describes three large longitudinal studies as outstanding (Barker-Lunn, 1970; Goldberg *et al*, 1966; Borg, 1965). Patterns found in Goldberg's research favoured broad mixed-ability groupings for all pupils except the most gifted, who did equally well in classes with broad or narrow ranges of ability. Slavin considers that this study 'is arguably the best evidence in existence against the possibility that reductions in IQ heterogeneity can enhance student achievement in the upper elementary grades. The size and rigor of the experiment make it highly unlikely that any nontrivial positive effect of ability grouping could have been missed ... those differences that were statistically significant support heterogeneous rather than ability-grouped class assignments'. The Barker-Lunn study found no meaningful trends favouring streamed or non-streamed schools. Slavin's comment is that 'again, if there were any consistent effect of ability-grouped class assignment on students' achievement, a study the size and quality of Barker-Lunn's would be very likely to find it'. Borg found that ability grouping was beneficial for the achievement of high-IQ pupils, detrimental for that of low-IQ pupils, and neutral for average-IQ pupils. However, Slavin cautions that Borg's evidence is less conclusive than that presented by Goldberg and Barker-Lunn because only two school districts were involved (so that district differences other than those connected with pupil groupings interfered) and because there was a greater proportion of high-IQ pupils in the district that grouped heterogeneously.

Hartill (1936) found that low-IQ pupils achieved slightly better in ability-grouped classes, high-IQ pupils achieved slightly better in mixed-ability classes, and average-IQ pupils did equally well in either grouping. Overall, achievement gains were identical in both groupings. Rankin *et al* (1936) found very small achievement differences (in favour of ability groupings) between ability groups and the heterogeneous classes. Daniels (1961), who compared two pairs of schools in England, and groups of pupils with matched IQ within them, found that pupils in the unstreamed schools were achieving at 'a significantly higher level' than those in the streamed school. Other multi-year studies (Breidenstine, 1936; Tobin, 1966) found effects near zero and Morgenstern (1963) found a small benefit of ability grouping. Loomer (1962) found no achievement benefits of a modified ability grouping plan in which high and average achievers were mixed and average and low achievers were mixed.

Some studies correlated the degrees to which classes were mixed with pupils' achievement: Justman (1968) found third graders' reading achievement increased slightly in mixed-ability classes, with average and low-achievers gaining the most. Leiter (1983) found no correlation between ability classes and achievement in reading or mathematics, but there was a nonsignificant trend towards higher reading achievement and lower maths achievement. Edminston and Benfer (1949) found that pupils in classes with a wide range of ability gained more in overall achievement than those in classes with a narrow ability range.

Slavin's comment on the research he reviewed is that 'given the persistence of the practice over time and the belief teachers typically place in its effectiveness, it is surprising to see how unequivocally the research evidence refutes the assertion that ability-grouped class assignment can increase student achievement in elementary schools'. The claim made in 'earlier reviews' (Begle, 1975; Eash, 1961; Esposito, 1973) that ability grouping is beneficial for high-ability pupils and detrimental for low-ability pupils was not supported by Slavin's own review; Slavin wonders whether it was the inclusion in these earlier reviews of studies for special programs for the gifted and for low achievers that made the difference. Slavin's conclusion from the literature on streaming in primary schools is that evidence from 17 comparisons, in thirteen matched equivalent and one randomised study, shows that streaming pupils according to general achievement or ability does not enhance their achievement in the elementary school.

Classroom observation studies

In our section on methodology, we made the point that variables other than school groupings *per se* are likely to influence pupil achievement, among them the impact of different teaching methods, the quality of teaching, teacher expectations, pupil expectations and sometimes different materials. Meticulously as Slavin's review (1987) was carried out, it has been criticised (Gamoran, 1987) for taking no account of variables such as these. We now move to a number of studies which have made one or more of these their focus. Notable among them is the review of observational studies undertaken by Good and Marshall (1984). One of the studies reviewed, that of Schwartz (1981), provides evidence of a likely link between teacher attitudes and expectations, and pupil behaviour.

Schwartz' work was carried out in three elementary schools and one junior high school, all operating a system of streaming by ability. Low-stream classes were characterised by disruptive behaviour and lack of peer interaction that supported learning. When these pupils were engaged on individual tasks their interactions were about social and personal events. In contrast, the high-stream pupils were more often on task and facilitated each others' efforts. The conclusion was that 'tracking in this study was associated with a peer culture that promoted academic goals in high-track classes but impeded them in low-ability classes'. The same study showed that, compared with the more able pupils, teachers made fewer demands on lower-stream pupils, made briefer comments on the pupils' report cards, and complained more about lower-ability pupils, but that they did not follow through discipline procedures as they did with the more able pupils. Good and Marshall concluded from their review of observational studies that there is little justification for streaming in primary (or lower secondary) schools.

Streaming and social class

The review of research into streaming and mixed-ability grouping undertaken by Gregory (1984) is of particular interest as Gregory's point of view was that of an educational psychologist working closely with a number of schools. Gregory quotes a number of studies which suggest that not only is there no evidence that streaming improves the attainment of children from lower social groups, but also that the achievement differences between children from lower- and middle-class social backgrounds continue to widen with time, whether or not pupils are streamed. Research undertaken by Davie *et al* (1972), Fogelman (1975) and Douglas *et al* (1968) showed that children from the lower social classes and larger families continued to have lower attainment than those from higher social classes and smaller families, whether they were aged seven or fifteen. Douglas and others showed that the achievement gap between children of different backgrounds continued to widen as they progressed through school (Douglas, 1964; Ross and Simpson, 1971; Fogelman and Goldstein, 1976).

There is some evidence to suggest that even with the advent of more mixed-ability grouping the pattern of middle-class children doing better than lower-class children is maintained. Using data gathered between 1965 and 1974 (a time when there was much change from streaming to mixed-ability grouping in primary and secondary schools in Britain) Essen, Fogelman and Ghodsian (1978) found that two-thirds of those with high maths and reading scores at age seven had high scores at 11, that three-quarters of those who had high scores at age eleven had high scores at age 16, and that similar figures held for those with the lowest scores. There was some movement, however, and generally children had a better chance of moving from the lowest to the highest score in primary school, rather than after age eleven in secondary school.

These findings suggest that factors other than pupil groupings are exerting an influence. Slavin's comments (1987) on the Barker-Lunn study (1970) made no reference to the social and attitudinal implications of the findings. Gregory, however, notes that Barker-Lunn found a deterioration in the reading performance of children from lower social classes compared with the performance of those from higher classes, and that she attributed this to teacher bias in favour of the higher social class children, teachers over-estimating the abilities of the higher class children and under-estimating those from lower social classes. Barker-Lunn also found that:

- teachers who favoured streaming (interestingly, and as noted earlier, these were slightly in the majority in the mixed-ability schools) tended to use more traditional methods and favour A-stream children and academic work, while teachers who favoured mixed-ability groupings tended to use progressive teaching methods, to be less biased towards A-stream children, to be more permissive and tolerant of noise, and to disapprove of the 11+ examination

- streamed schools most commonly used whole-class teaching and similar-ability grouping within the class

- mixed-ability schools most commonly used similar-ability grouping within the class and individual teaching, and nearly half the mixed-ability school teachers were streaming within their classrooms, with different tables for different abilities.

Gregory points out that the implication of this last finding may be that 'Barker-Lunn has not compared streamed and unstreamed classes but streaming between classes with streaming within classes'. If this point is accepted, then Barker-Lunn's finding that there were no meaningful trends favouring streamed or non-streamed schools may have to be re-evaluated. Barker-Lunn found no difference in the attainments of pupils taught by pro- or anti-streaming teachers, but Gregory points out that some of the anti-streaming teachers used ability groups within the class. The Barker-Lunn study also found that children of average and below-average ability showed better attitudes (their self-images, relationships with teachers and social adjustment) if they were in mixed-ability schools and taught by pro-mixed-ability teachers. (Children of above average ability tended to show such attitudes no matter what kind of school they were in.) Furthermore, children in streamed schools, particularly those of average and below-average ability, took less part in school activities than did the children in mixed-ability schools. Overall, Gregory concluded that the evidence of effects of streaming and mixed-ability grouping for both primary and secondary schools was inconclusive, and that while streaming had been abused in the past, mixed-ability grouping simply changed the problem.

Attitudes towards streaming

With some exceptions, most notably that of Barker-Lunn (1970), most of the research so far reviewed here has been North American in origin. However, that conducted by Lee and Croll (1995), who surveyed the prevalence of, and attitudes towards, streaming in two English education authorities, offers a more recent and British perspective. From their questionnaires to 246 headteachers, Lee and Croll found that recent practice contrasted sharply with that in the late 1960s when Barker-Lunn carried out her study and 'reported considerable difficulties in finding a sample of non-streamed schools for her study of the effects of streaming and non-streaming in primary schools'. In contrast, Lee and Croll found almost no streaming in the primary schools in the two authorities. This applied across all the school sizes represented in the survey, although such streaming as there was was more likely to be in the largest schools. However, Lee and Croll point out that views were more varied than practice, with about half the headteachers thinking that streaming did not have educational value for primary schools and almost 40% thinking it did. Of those who thought it did have value, the majority thought all children could benefit and a quarter that the most able would benefit, while only 6.5% thought there were benefits for the less able.

In spite of the relatively large minority of headteachers who believed that streaming had educational value, Lee and Croll found little evidence that they expected strong support for streaming from other interested groups: 'It is clear that heads do not, in general, experience parental pressure for the reintroduction of streaming'. Asked how feasible they thought it would be to introduce streaming into their schools, about two thirds of the headteachers said it would not be possible and about a third that it would. These perceptions were strongly influenced by school size, heads of large schools being more likely to think it possible to introduce streaming than those in small schools. However, because some headteachers from small schools thought streaming would be possible and some from large schools thought not, Lee and Croll conclude that factors other than school size were influencing them (eg complex school organisational arrangements set up to deal with unbalanced entries in different years).

Lee and Croll draw attention to the mismatch between practice and many headteachers' views, and comment on the degree of variation in professional opinion shown within 'an almost entirely non-streamed system'. In particular, they note that 'the proportion of headteachers expressing at least a degree of support for streaming is only 25% lower in the early 1990s than it was in the early 1960s'. They claim that the research supports the OfSTED notion (1993) that primary schools are willing to review their practices. Later experience shows that, in the event, this may be the case in relation to setting rather than streaming.

A study by Mason (1995) illustrates the dangers of assuming that mixed-ability school groupings mean that classes will be taught differently from streamed classes. From a survey of principals (headteachers) in twelve North American states, Mason found that most schools allocated pupils to mixed-ability classes, the majority using criteria such as IQ or previous reading achievement to ensure a mix, but some choosing the classes randomly. However, within their classrooms, teachers most often taught the class as a whole, although the frequency dropped a little as children grew older.

Setting
Recent trends
Although setting has been a common form of organisation of classes in secondary schools, it has not been widespread in primary schools, where ability grouping for particular subjects has been within-class rather than across classes. However it has recently been advocated as a means of improving standards in upper primary classes. Some have linked this trend to the introduction of the National Curriculum in England and Wales (Sukhnandan and Lee, 1998) and the 5–14 Guidelines in Scotland. The specification of what has to be learned has been associated with greater structure in the organisation of teaching and this has been seen as a justification for setting (Morrice, 1999).

An example of official approval of setting is found in Scotland, with its seven-year primary school, where a report by HM Inspectors has advised that in secondary schools, 'increased use of setting should make class management more feasible'. For primary schools the advice was less forceful and was that 'in large primary schools, with more than one class at each stage, the effectiveness of setting pupils in P6 and P7 for English and mathematics should be carefully considered'. In both cases, a main thrust of the rationale for setting is that it reduces the time spent on organising and managing learning to allow more time for 'direct teaching'. The term 'direct teaching' is interpreted widely by HMI in the *Achievement for All* report (SOEID, 1996); indeed it is defined in terms of many of the characteristics of effective teaching, including:
- varied questioning of pupils and giving clear explanations in a range of contexts

- listening and responding to pupils' answers and views
- sharing objectives with pupils when setting tasks which challenge and motivate
- monitoring the progress and pace of learning of individuals within groups
- responding to individual needs by identifying next steps in learning. (SOEID, 1996)

Teaching with these characteristics clearly requires more teacher-pupil interaction. This can only happen if there is more whole-class teaching since group or individual teaching necessarily means that those not in the group being taught are working on their own. When this happens for long periods, time on task is reduced (McPake *et al*, forthcoming) and achievement suffers (Brophy and Good, 1986).

The potential for setting, as for streaming, is limited by the size of the school and the number of staff available. In many cases, setting will not reduce the range of ability by very much. Thus, in some sets, there will be the same disadvantages for pupils for whom whole-class teaching is the norm as have been reported for whole-class teaching with mixed-ability classes, *viz.* that the needs of individual pupils are not addressed and that 'there is a danger that the faster learner will not feel challenged and become bored, while slower children feel frustrated and experience a sense of failure' (Edwards and Woodhead, 1996, p5). The solution is to create groups within the set so that greater differentiation in teaching can be provided. In this way the main benefit for the teacher is that there is a reduced range of ability among the groups. It may thus be possible to minimise the number of groups and maximise opportunities for 'direct teaching'.

Whilst there is clear evidence that the practice of setting in primary schools in England is increasing, this is a trend too recent to have much sustained research as its focus. A 1998 report from OfSTED based on HMI evidence indicated an increase in prevalence of setting in the upper primary school (ten and eleven year-olds) in England with about 60% of junior schools teaching pupils in sets for at least one subject, most frequently in mathematics. Just under a quarter of the Year Six mathematics classes (eleven year-olds) observed by the inspectors in 1997 were being taught in sets. The inspectors found that 'the vast majority of headteachers and teachers in these schools reported that standards in setted subjects are higher and the quality of education provided is better, than was the case before setting was introduced' (OfSTED, 1998, p 5). Teachers and headteachers in the schools where setting was practised liked it, and considered that it had a positive effect on the quality of education. Although pupils invariably knew the relative ranking of their set, there was no evidence of resentment or demotivation on this account.

Nevertheless, the inspectors identified evidence of differentiated quality of teaching for the high- and low-ability sets. Teaching quality was highest in the upper sets and, for mathematics, 'the least effective teaching was seen in lower sets, whilst in English and science the weakest teaching was found in middle sets where three or more sets had been formed'. The reason for this difference was that help from the Special Educational Needs coordinator was often deployed in the lowest English set. The inspectors expressed particular concern about the weakness of lower set mathematics teaching 'given that in many schools one of the stated intentions of setting is to help raise the performance of the lowest attaining pupils' (p6). This lends force to the inspectors' caution that setting, *per se*, cannot 'guarantee success in raising standards'.

Studies of setting and achievement

We identified relatively little research with setting at primary school level as its focus. Again, Slavin's review of 1987 is a major contributor to the debate, though it must be noted that all the research he reviewed was from the United States, that 'regrouping', the form of setting that he reviews, was always for reading and/or maths, and that regrouping may not have an exact equivalent in Britain. Slavin's view is that this form of grouping can be expected to produce more homogeneity than ability grouping by class because (1) the presumed negative psychological effects of class grouping are minimised; (2) regrouping is done on the basis of actual performance in reading or mathematics, not IQ; (3) the grouping is relatively flexible – pupils can move from group to group more easily.

The seven studies of regrouping that Slavin included in his review present a mixed picture, with five of the seven finding that pupils learned more in regrouped than in mixed-ability classes, and two finding the opposite. Those by Koontz (1961), Balow and Ruddell (1963) and Morris (1969) investigated the effects of regrouping in both reading and mathematics. Koontz found negative effects in both subjects but especially for reading, while there were gains for those in self-contained mixed-ability classes. Balow and Ruddell found positive effects in both reading and mathematics for average and for below-average achievers. Morris found that overall pupil achievement was higher in regrouped classes for reading and maths than in mixed-ability control groups.

Two of the studies looked only at reading: Moses (1966) found no consistent difference in reading achievement, but Berkun, Swanson and Sawyer (1966) found significantly greater gains for regrouping than self-contained reading classes. However, Slavin points out that there are methodological problems with this study.

Slavin notes that Provus (1960) 'provides the best evidence in favour' of regrouping for mathematics, finding that achievement gains for high-ability students in the regrouping program were much greater than those of comparable control students, but the program was 'less spectacularly beneficial' for average and low-ability students. In contrast, Davis and Tracy (1963) found regrouping for mathematics to be detrimental to pupils, but Slavin warns that this study was limited to two schools and that differentiated teaching materials were not used.

Slavin was unable to reach definite conclusions about the effectiveness of regrouping at primary school level as there were too few quality studies for this purpose. However, he clearly feels it to be important that research should take account of the use of differentiated teaching materials and teaching methods, commenting that though none of the patterns evaluated was consistently successful, the Provus study gave strong evidence favouring the use of regrouping in maths if pupils were given materials appropriate to their levels of performance, and that the Morris study also found strong positive effects of regrouping for reading and maths, with the suggestion that this was especially likely if the levels of instruction were adapted to accommodate pupil differences. Slavin concludes, 'these studies suggest that regrouping for reading and / or mathematics can be effective if instructional pace and materials are adapted to students' needs, whereas simply regrouping without extensively adapting materials or regrouping in all academic subjects is ineffective'.

The study by Mason (1995), already noted in reference to streaming, was conducted through a survey of 571 primary school headteachers in twelve North American states. Mason was not concerned with the effects of different groupings but with their prevalence and the way that they were made up. He found it uncommon for schools to set for mathematics in the lower age grades; having been allocated to mixed-ability classes, pupils tended to remain in these classes for maths, taught by their 'home-room teachers' on a whole class basis. Setting for maths grew more common as pupils grew older, however, (though it was still a minority practice) and by sixth grade over a quarter of the schools regrouped in this way. Teachers from traditional schools were reported as more likely to use setting than were teachers in less traditional schools. This is not unexpected since setting is easier to implement where there is a strict timetable for different subjects than in schools with a less formal structure. In the latter case time is likely to be consumed in coordinating the regrouping across classes.

Setting and social class

Gregory (1984) cites Project Follow-Through in America as evidence in favour of setting, in particular the success of one of its programs, DISTAR, which is said to have 'raised the attainments of economically disadvantaged, backward, primary-aged children to average American norms in four years' (Becker, 1977). The program was taught to groups of six to ten children with similar instructional needs. Gregory attributes its success, at least in part, to the programme authors' assumption that 'intelligent behaviour can be learnt and that backward children can 'catch up' academically if taught appropriately... The belief that one can improve the intelligence and attainments of such pupils immediately raises the expectations one has for their future performance'. However, Project Follow-Through programmes were designed to improve the attainment levels of children with special educational needs, and as such would have been eliminated from reviews such as that of Slavin (1987).

Cross-age grouping

Slavin's review includes a section on the Joplin and similar plans. These are specialised forms of setting for reading, an important feature of which is that they are 'non-graded', ie they include pupils from different age groups. Although such plans in their original form are specific to American schools, the findings have relevance to setting in small primary schools where two or more year groups are combined in the setted classes. The studies in the US were, according to Slavin, remarkably consistent in favouring the cross-grading setting. In eleven out of fourteen studies, the quality of which were in Slavin's view very high, Joplin Plan or similar groupings achieved more than mixed-ability classes; the other three studies found no differences. Overall, the advantages do not seem to be associated with pupils of any particular ability, and Slavin points out that in no case did one subgroup gain at the expense of another: either all ability levels gained more than their control counterparts, or none did. Slavin adds that, though positive effects of the Joplin Plan might be due to the novelty of the approach, some of the studies with the largest effects lasted three years (eg Hart, 1962; Ingram, 1960; Skapski, 1960).

An alternative way of reducing the range of ability, with an element of cross-age grouping, has been proposed by Prais (1997), supported by research evidence from testing pupils in classes in Switzerland and England. Prais noted that in classes in Switzerland there is a reduced range of ability because the slower learning pupils in each year group are taught with the year below, either having entered school a year later or having repeated a class. He measured the attainment in mathematics of pupils in 15 classes in England, average age ten years, and compared the results with the scores on the same test of pupils in four classes, average age nine years, in Switzerland. The average score of the Swiss pupils was slightly higher than that of the English pupils, even though the Swiss pupils had completed just under three years of school whilst the English pupils had completed just under five years. However, the difference in the range of attainments was an even more startling finding: the variability in scores of the English pupils' was about twice that of the Swiss class. Prais comments that:

> It is not surprising in the light of these disparities, that many English teachers have decided that a better rate of learning requires them to divide their pupils, even at these young ages, into three attainment groups...   (Prais, 1997, p283)

He implies that if the variability of the English class could be reduced then more whole-class teaching would be possible and that in the longer-term, variability would be further reduced due to the 'benefits arising from the more manageable nature of the class that faces teachers in such circumstances' (p284). Prais calculates that it would only take the transfer of the lowest three pupils in each class to reduce the variability in the English classes three-quarters of the way to the Swiss level.

Within-class grouping
Forms of grouping
It has already been noted that in many studies where setting or streaming was compared with mixed-ability teaching, there was ability grouping within the mixed-ability class. Bealing's survey of 1971 found widespread use of within-class ability grouping for mathematics and language work in non-streamed and non-setted schools (Bealing, 1972), and this has continued as the most common pattern of class organisation in primary schools in the UK throughout the 1970s and 1980s.

In reviewing research on the effect of within-class grouping on achievement, it is necessary to distinguish between the formation of smaller teaching groups in order to reduce the number of pupils the teacher has to deal with at any one time, although all groups may experience much the same teaching, and the formation of *ability* groups which are treated differently according to what they have already achieved. Classes also differ in respect of whether pupils stay in their ability groups to do all the work set in the particular subject, or, as in many classrooms, receive direct instruction in ability groups but when carrying out work set by the teacher (whilst the teacher interacts with other groups) return to sit in mixed-ability groups. This has implications for the degree of cooperative learning that can take place when the pupils are working on the tasks assigned to them.

Within-class grouping and attainment

In the studies comparing within-class ability grouping with whole-class teaching there is unequivocal evidence for the effectiveness of within-class *ability* grouping in raising the achievement of all pupils (eg Dewar, 1964; Smith, 1960; Spence, 1958), particularly for low achievers (Stern, 1972). More significant than the findings of individual studies are the outcomes of an extensive and carefully conducted meta-analysis of studies of within-class grouping by Lou *et al* (1996). Their analysis of 51 studies showed that 'on average, students learning in small groups within classrooms achieved significantly more than students not learning in small groups' (Lou *et al*, 1996, p439). However these studies included both those in which the teaching and materials were adapted to the small groups and those where the treatment was the same as in the whole-class situation. When these were separated, the researchers found that there were significant differences between the whole-class and small-class arrangements *only* when there were differences in the treatments given in the two situations. Thus the effect of grouping appears to result from the way in which teaching is adapted to the groups rather than just to the physical situation in which the pupils are learning. This echoes the finding that setting is not effective unless materials and pace are adapted for the classes of different ability.

The meta-analysis of Lou *et al* found that the effect sizes were greatest when groups were formed on the basis of ability specific to the subject being taught, but with other information taken into account (subject ability alone was no more effective than using general ability as a basis for grouping). Low and high ability pupils were the ones to gain most. Group size was also a relevant factor, a size of three or four being optimum.

Some studies investigated difference in attitudes related to grouping. Overall these indicated that within-class grouping was positively related to attitudes to the subject but that there was no significant difference in other attitudes or in self-concept.

Further light was thrown on the effect of group composition by the meta-analysis by Lou *et al* of twelve studies of within-class grouping in which mixed-ability groups were compared with ability groups. The results indicated 'a slight superiority of homogenous ability groups over heterogeneous ability groups in promoting student achievement' (p445). The pupils to gain most from this were those of medium ability. Low-ability pupils gained most from mixed-ability groups, whilst the group composition made only a small difference for the high-ability pupils. The effects were particularly strong in reading and negligible for mathematics and science.

Reasons for the differential effect of ability grouping on medium-ability pupils were offered by Askew and Wiliam (1995) in terms of group interactions:

> There is substantial evidence that the extent to which a pupil gives detailed explanations is a good predictor of how much pupils will benefit from small-group working. Not surprisingly, it is the higher-achieving pupils that do more explaining when working in a mixed-ability group and so gain most. In mixed-ability groups it is the lower-attaining pupils who ask the most questions. Hence in groups with a wide spread of attainment, the middle-attainers miss out, as they neither seek nor give help.
>
> (Askew and Wiliam, 1995, p38)

These authors go on to claim that in groups with a narrow range of attainment, there is less asking for and giving of help. This would appear not to explain the finding of Lou *et al* that middle-ability pupils have most to gain from within-class ability grouping. However, it may also be that the absence of the higher and lower ability pupils from the group gives them a chance to address queries at their own level. All of these explanations presuppose some group interaction about the learning task, but classroom observation shows that this is not a common feature of classroom work, as we will now see.

Classroom observation of within-class grouping
Classroom observations (McPake *et al*, 1999) have shown that task-based interaction is infrequent and often explicitly discouraged by teachers who ask pupils to attend to their own work only, or is

implicitly prevented by seating arrangements which require the pupils to sit in groups of different ability when working on their assignments, so that they do not have tasks in common with their neighbours.

McPake *et al* found that genuinely collaborative work, where there is cooperative learning towards a combined group outcome, was particularly rare, but when it did occur there was a very high proportion of time on task. Evidence that this is likely to lead to higher achievement was provided by Lou and colleagues (1996) who examined the effect of the type of instruction experienced by small groups in different studies. They found that small groups working collaboratively achieved significantly more than other groups not working towards a combined outcome.

Most of the observational studies of ability grouping reviewed by Good and Marshall (1984) concerned younger pupils learning to read. However there are points of general relevance. For example:

- low-ability readers grouped together tend to interrupt each other
- a greater variety of reading books is used with the more able readers
- teachers emphasised comprehension for the high-ability groups but decoding skills for the low-ability readers to the neglect of meaning
- teachers discouraged interruptions of a pupil reading aloud with the high-ability groups but not with the low-ability ones
- low-ability pupils were allowed less time to correct their own mistakes before the teacher or other pupils intervened to supply the correction
- being placed in a high reading group was found by Weinstein (1976) to have a positive effect on achievement.

The value of small groups for teaching reading was acknowledged, but these need not be based on ability. Moreover, the basis for grouping was tenuous and more often based on perceived general ability/maturity than on specific reading skills and this often meant that social background was an important factor.

Observational studies of the teacher seem to indicate that a vicious circle can be created when there is ability grouping: pupils in low-ability groups feel stigmatised and demotivated; teachers are less motivated to teach them and have lower expectations of them; in turn, this reduces the opportunities for achievement, and pupils in low-ability groups tend to stay there. The stability of groups suggests that not all children are learning at the optimum rate. A further effect on the teacher is that there may be an assumption that a homogeneous group will have understood because they have all been taught the same thing, with, as a consequence, less incentive to use continuous assessment to ascertain pupils' learning. Teachers of heterogeneous groups or classes are more likely to conduct continuous assessment and to try to ensure that all pupils are developing understanding.

The message that seems to emerge from these observational studies is that it benefits lower-ability pupils to have opportunities to learn with the more able even if at some times they are taught separately to make the class easier to handle.

The work of Simpson *et al* (1989) underlines the point that grouping by ability will not improve pupils' opportunities to learn unless teachers cater effectively for individual differences. These researchers made independent judgements of the match between the capabilities of the pupils observed and the level of demand of the tasks they were given. They found a good match for less than a half of the pupils in the top and middle-ability groups, with over half of the top groups being under-challenged. Middle and lower-attaining pupils were frequently 'allocated work in areas where they were not able to show understanding or competence in simpler or pre-requisite skills'. In order to improve the match, the teachers themselves identified the need for better information about pupils' progression in various areas of skills and understanding, more effective ways of handling this information, and time – time to collect better information about pupils by observing and listening, and time to reflect upon and use the information.

Attainment in mathematics
All the eight studies of within-class ability grouping that Slavin (1987) included in his review were concerned with achievement in maths, although one (Jones, 1948) also covered reading and spelling. Slavin's review, therefore, provides substantial evidence of the effects

of within-class ability grouping on achievement in maths. Every study favoured it, though not always significantly. Low achievers appeared to gain the most: Slavin notes that the median effect size for these pupils was higher than for average or high achievers. Two of the studies were conducted by Slavin himself together with Karweit (Slavin and Karweit, 1985). These were large randomised studies, one in mixed-ability schools, the other in relatively homogeneous schools. The first compared a form of non-traditional whole-class instruction with within-class ability grouping using two groups. Results from the semester-long study indicated significantly higher achievement in ability groups compared with whole-class instruction. The second study, which made the same comparisons, achieved similar results.

Among the other randomised studies included in Slavin's review was that of Dewar (1964), who randomly assigned sixth grade mathematics classes (eleven year-olds) and their teachers to use within-class ability grouping or whole-class teaching for a full school year, with results that strongly favoured the grouped classes for pupils who had been in the top, middle and low groups in comparison to their counterparts in the control group. In a shorter but otherwise similar study conducted with children from grades two to five (age seven to ten), Smith (1960) also found results which favoured within-class ability groupings, especially for pupils assigned to the lowest group. Wallen and Vowles (1960) reported the smallest positive effect of any study of within-class ability grouping. For one semester they randomly assigned sixth grade mathematics pupils to ability or whole-class groups, then for the second semester they reversed the arrangement so that pupils previously in ability groups were taught as a whole class and vice versa. Higher first semester scores for the ability-grouped pupils were nearly wiped out in the second semester.

Slavin reports that three non-randomised studies supported the results of the randomised ones described above. Spence (1958) found significantly greater gains for the within-class ability-grouped pupils. Stern (1972) focused on the lowest 20% ability range, with gain scores clearly favouring the grouped classes in spite of pre-test differences which favoured the control pupils. Jones (1948) found that grouped classes for reading, spelling and mathematics were favoured for all three subjects and for all three levels of ability studies.

Summarising, Slavin points out that the research consistently supports within-class ability grouping in the upper elementary grades, and that this research is of exceptional quality; but he warns that there was not enough research on within-class ability grouping in reading, or in the lower primary years, to permit conclusions. No gains were made at the expense of low achievers, who were the greatest gainers if anything. Slavin thinks the novelty effect is unlikely, as within-class grouping is an established practice.

With reference to his own work (1984), Slavin (1987) raises a further point in relation to teacher-pupil interaction. He points out that when a teacher uses a within-class ability group plan with three groups, the pupils must spend at least two-thirds of the available teaching time working without direct teacher support, and comments that several studies have found that a large amount of unsupervised seat-work is detrimental to pupil achievement (eg Brophy and Good, 1986). Furthermore, transition between ability groups further reduces the available teaching time (Arlin, 1979). These points lead Slavin to recommend that there should be no more than three groups within a class.

Pros and cons of within-class grouping

While Slavin's review concentrated on determining how far pupil achievement was affected by different groupings, McNamara and Waugh (1993) explored the literature for evidence of other kinds of advantage and disadvantage to be found in within-class groupings. They state that a shift away from whole-class teaching can be justified on the grounds of learning theory (Bereiter, 1972; Smith, 1986), social arguments (Jackson, 1964; Barker-Lunn, 1970) and promoting the most effective learning conditions for pupils (Cumbria County Council, 1988; Corson, 1987; Dougill and Knott, 1988).

In addition, McNamara and Waugh note there are many studies investigating grouping in primary classrooms and the learning/teaching practices associated with them (Bennett *et al*, 1976; Galton *et al*, 1980; Calfee and Piontowski, 1987; Thomas, 1987; Wilkinson, 1988–89; Mortimore *et al*, 1988; Evertson, 1989; Alexander, 1991).

They summarise the major findings from this research as being that:

- The most common form of class grouping is homogeneous, based on some index of ability.

  – In effect this means that children are streamed within the class, in spite of the mixed-ability aim of overcoming the divisive effects of streaming.

  – Children know whether they are in high or low groups.

  – To organise groups according to one measure of ability does not ensure homogeneity for learning purposes.

- When children are grouped for one educational purpose it may be that other purposes are confounded, eg friendship groups tend to group boys with boys and girls with girls, so gender barriers are being maintained.

- Teachers cannot assume that children will work well just because they are in groups; they are likely to need group skills.

  – Nor can teachers assume that because children are in groups they will work cooperatively – the work they carry out while in groups has not been observed to require cooperative behaviour and the evidence further suggests that children work best in groups when they undertake clear-cut assignments which are closely monitored by the teacher.

  – If children organised into groups carry out tasks which do not require group organisation, teachers need to ask if the added effort of organising the classroom appropriately is worth it.

- Less able and disadvantaged children are disadvantaged in group settings because the more able children have the skills to cope with less structured learning situations and are more likely to be motivated to work assiduously without supervision.

- Group size is often determined by the room and the furniture arrangements rather than by educational goals.

McNamara and Waugh point out that other research (Alexander, 1991; Desforges and Cockburn, 1986; Galton *et al*, 1980) shows that managerial problems for the teacher are exacerbated if children in different groups are engaged in different activities.

Summary

- Streaming in primary schools was largely abandoned in the 1960s for reasons related to social equality; although headteachers are not fundamentally opposed to it, there has been no large movement for its re-introduction.

- Setting was less common in the past but is being advocated in order to reduce the range of ability in a class and so make possible more 'direct teaching', which must involve more whole-class teaching.

- The research into the effects of streaming and setting on pupils' achievement provides no evidence of overall effect; gains for one ability group tend to be off-set by losses for another.

- Observation studies of streamed classes revealed a work-oriented peer culture in high-ability classes and a peer culture that impeded achievement in low-ability classes; recent inspectors' reports have noted that the least effective teaching was found in middle and lowest sets.

- Cross-age grouping is an alternative way of reducing the range of ability in a teaching group and allows more whole-class teaching.

- Grouping within a class is a common form of organisation to reduce the size of teaching groups, but the greater the number of groups, the more time pupils have to spend working on their own whilst teachers are talking to other groups.

- When within-class groups are formed on the basis of ability in the subject being taught, there are advantages for all pupils providing that teaching materials and pace are adapted to the pupils' needs.

- The greatest gains for within-class ability grouping are found in mathematics; in reading, evidence is less clear and observation studies show that low-ability readers fare better in mixed-ability groups.

3

Secondary School Level

Setting and streaming

We noted at the beginning of Chapter 2 that, almost without exception, secondary schools were streamed up to the 1960s. Moreover, not only was their intake differentiated by ability but in many cases pupils were streamed within the schools by general ability and also reorganised into sets for specific subjects, particularly mathematics and foreign languages. The evidence that sorting pupils by ability in these ways was disadvantaging large numbers of pupils and was particularly holding back those of working-class background (for example Hargreaves, 1967; Lacy, 1970) added weight to the political move to promote greater equity in educational opportunities. Large areas of Britain adopted non-selective comprehensive secondary schooling and the same thinking and values led to streaming within schools being widely discontinued.

The relative merits of mixed-ability and ability groups, formed by setting or streaming, have largely been argued in terms of social and attitudinal outcomes. The research evidence, as we shall see, gives little clear indication that achievement overall is improved by teaching pupils in homogeneous or heterogeneous groups based on ability. Any benefits for the higher attainers have been found to be offset by disbenefits for the lower attainers.

It is difficult to account for the return to favour of setting that has been seen in the 1990s in Britain in terms of demonstrable improvements in standards overall. Popular opinion that ability grouping improves achievement fails to take into account the differences that exist, in several very relevant factors, between those schools which divide pupils by ability and those which do not. These factors include difference in ethos, approach to teaching and learning and, where there is parental choice, background of intake. It is relatively easy to find schools which stream and set and have high exam results and those which have lower results and practise mixed-ability teaching. But when these school variables are controlled, any differences which are due to ability grouping often disappear.

However, it may be that, as Boaler (1997c) has suggested, the introduction of national curricula and other reforms arising directly and indirectly from the Education Reform Act (ERA) 1988 forced schools 'to turn their primary attention away from equality and towards academic success, particularly for the most able' (Boaler, 1997c, p576). Boaler quotes research of Gewirtz *et al* (1993) as evidence that teachers considered the National Curriculum for England and Wales to be incompatible with mixed-ability teaching. Be that as it may, it is certainly the case that the ERA and its Scottish counterpart heralded a curriculum in which targets for achievement were set and associated assessment put in place, providing a ready mechanism for dividing pupils by attainment. When the requirements of target-setting are added and schools put under pressure to raise the proportion of pupils reaching certain levels, it is not surprising if pupils just below these levels are separated and given special attention. These combinations of factors appear to have initiated a return to setting which has been explicitly encouraged by official sources (Blair, 1996; SOEID, 1999).

In the United States there appears to have been an increase in the prevalence of streaming. Survey data from the late 1980s (Epstein and MacIver, 1990) showed that 20% of schools with grades seven and eight ('middle' or lower secondary) practised streaming and over 40% used some form of setting, mostly for English and mathematics. In 1993, a further survey found 82% of middle-level schools using some form of ability grouping. This change is in conflict with the lack of evidence of the effectiveness of ability grouping and with the unequivocal recommendations of the Carnegie Council on Adolescent Development (1989) that all tracking by ability should be eliminated. The document described tracking as one of the most divisive and damaging school practices in existence.

In his review of student achievement and ability grouping in secondary schools, Slavin (1990) makes no major distinction between setting and streaming, and in practice these are often found in combination. Here we therefore deal with both of these forms of ability grouping together, pointing out differences where significant and important. The main distinction is between classes selected by ability and mixed-ability classes for teaching. We deal separately, necessarily briefly, with within-class grouping in secondary schools.

Studies of effects on overall achievement

Slavin's 1990 review covered 29 studies which met the 'best-evidence' criteria summarised earlier (see page 10) for his review of elementary schools. However, twelve of these studies focused on pupils at grade nine or above (aged 14 or older). As we are concerned with research into streaming and setting in the early years of the secondary school, specific comment on the findings from these studies has been omitted from the current review. Overall, Slavin found that there were no effects of ability grouping on pupil achievement, for any levels of ability. The great majority of the studies reviewed showed zero effect sizes for different ability groups, and although Slavin notes that the group of highest quality studies (those in which students were randomised or matched) provided slightly more support for the idea that ability grouping has a positive differential effect, he stresses that 'the study by Borg (1965), which is often cited to support the differential effect of ability grouping on students of different ability levels, in fact provides very weak support for this phenomenon'. Differences in study location (eg Britain, Sweden and the USA) showed no consistent patterns, and in fact Slavin comments that there were few consistent patterns in the study findings overall.

Gregory (1984), reviewing the evidence for and against streaming compared with mixed-ability in secondary schools, reported contradictory findings with respect to pupil achievement:

- mixed-ability grouping marginally favours children aged eleven to twelve (Goldberg *et al*, 1966)
- streaming favours children of eleven but there is no difference between ages twelve to sixteen (Svenson, 1965)
- there is no difference in the effects of mixed-ability and streaming (Thompson, 1974; Newbold, 1977; Rudd, 1956; Fogelman *et al*, 1978; Winn *et al*, 1983)

- there was no difference in exam results for pupils, some of whom had experienced mixed-ability grouping and some of whom had experienced streaming in their earlier years at secondary school, though all were streamed subsequently (Postlethwaite and Denton, 1978)
- the less able pupils performed better in mixed-ability classes (Postlethwaite and Denton, 1978) .

Gregory concludes that 'the evidence about the effects of streaming/ setting or mixed-ability grouping in secondary school on attainment, social adjustment or friendship patterns is equivocal and inconclusive. It is probably safest to conclude that there are no differences.'

Effects on different ability groups
Within the overall picture of no effects of ability grouping, Slavin found some slight evidence of benefits for low-achieving pupils: Torgelson (1963) found non-significant differences in favour of ability grouping for low-achieving grades seven to nine. However, grouping high achievers together seems to have no effect except when curriculum materials in advance of those usually considered appropriate for the age group are used (Fox, 1979; Kulik and Kulik, 1984).

Slavin concludes that 'taken together, research comparing ability-grouped to heterogeneous placements provides little support for the proposition that high achievers gain from grouping whereas low achievers lose'. However, he comments that often streaming guides pupils to different courses (eg metalwork for vocational courses, a modern language for academic courses) and that these require different types of preparation. These differences will give rise to different effects and the studies he summarised in the review do not take account of them.

Askew and Wiliam (1995) drew the following from a review of research of grouping on high attainers in mathematics:

- the greatest gains were found when their study materials were particularly written for high attainers
- it was, consequently, not clear whether it was the materials and teacher attention or the grouping that caused the benefit

- high attainers gained as much from mixed-ability collaborative work as any other pupils.

Boaler, however, reported a sharp difference between boys and girls in high ability mathematics sets. Many top-set girls were 'unhappy because they felt that the pace of lessons was too fast, which often caused them to become anxious about work and to fall behind; this caused them to become more anxious' (Boaler, 1997c, p581). But it is not only the top sets and the girls who disliked working at a fixed pace. All the students interviewed from Year 9 (age 14) onwards, complained about having to work at the same pace as the class and compared it adversely with their earlier experience of working at their own pace in mixed-ability classes. The students studied by Boaler were in a large secondary school, with eight sets in the year 'which should produce relatively little variation amongst students in the same set'. Boaler suggests that the fact that this did not appear to be the case may reflect the fact that 'the ability of a student does not necessarily indicate the pace they feel comfortable working at, although this is an assumption that class teaching to setted groups is predicated upon' (p 582). She pointed out that the aspect of setting that students disliked the most – teaching at the same pace for all in the set – was the central rationale for advocating setting. Her interviews with students showed that they considered learning was reduced by a common pace. They regretted the lack of individual help which they had experienced in earlier years in mixed-ability classes.

Research by Eilam and Finegold (1992) threw light on the effect of the range of differences within mixed-ability classes. They studied the progress of pupils in heterogeneous classes in a junior high school in Israel taking in pupils with a very wide range of socio-economic, cultural and academic backgrounds. Their focus was on the gap between the advantaged and disadvantaged pupils, a gap which was not diminished during the three years of the study. They found that disadvantaged pupils were relatively more successful in the classes with the least gap between the advantaged and disadvantaged. It was noted, however, that 'despite the school's policy of integration based on heterogeneous classes and the academic support system, individual teachers made little effort to change their traditional style of teaching to suit the needs of the heterogeneous class and to implement active academic and social class interactions' (Eilam and Finegold, 1992, p176).

Studies of social and behavioural effects

Watson (1985) reviewed evidence against the practice of streaming, finding that this included the following:

- the less able feel discouraged when segregated from the able (Kelly, 1975)
- there are no advantages for low-IQ children in being placed in special classes (Calberg and Kavale, 1980; Frampton, no date)
- non-streaming has positive effects on academic performance at both ends of the ability range (Thompson, 1974)
- there is no significant difference in the performance of pupils in mixed and ability groups (McPhee, 1978).

At the same time there is research to show that mixed-ability organisation leads to social advantages without academic disadvantages, and some gain for low-ability pupils in mixed-ability classes. Watson cites Newbold (1977) who took part in a longitudinal study in a large school where pupils were allocated to four 'Halls', and the organisation of the Halls was varied from year to year. Two of the four ran mixed-ability classes in the first year while first year classes in the two others were streamed. In the second year, one Hall remained mainly mixed-ability while the others were streamed; in the third year both the Halls that had begun with mixed-ability groupings were setted on the basis of ability in each subject. The first phase of the study concluded that mixed-ability organisation leads to social advantages without academic disadvantages, with some gain for low-ability pupils in mixed-ability classes; and the final conclusion was that 'both the most and least able from the mixed-ability group appeared to do slightly better academically in the final year of schooling' (Postlethwaite and Denton, 1978).

Other arguments in favour of mixed-ability classes were advanced by Whitehead *et al* (1977), who found that pupils in mixed-ability classes read more books than those in streamed classes, and by the Bullock Report (1975) which stressed that, in English classes especially, the less able needed the stimulus of other pupils and that the linguistically able needed opportunities to communicate with the less linguistically accomplished. The report also commented on the dangers inherent in assuming that streamed groups were homogeneous groups: 'Classifying individuals in this way makes different pupils in the same group seem more similar than they are, and similar pupils in different groups seem more different than they are'.

Gregory (1984) reported that research findings in terms of the discipline effects associated with streaming and mixed-ability grouping gave a somewhat mixed picture:

- some research finds in favour of streaming, some in favour of mixed-ability groups (Morrison, 1976)
- pupils are more likely to be rated ill-behaved in mixed-ability schools but those schools are less likely to develop delinquent sub-cultures and form especially difficult classes (Ross *et al*, 1972)
- teacher attitudes follow the streams, ie teachers see low-stream pupils as failures, low-stream pupils as delinquent (Hargreaves, 1967)
- social class affects aspirations – lowest aspirations are held by low social-class secondary modern pupils (Ferri, 1971).

A qualitative study by Spear (1994) explored teachers' thinking about ability grouping and found that those who retain ability grouping are more subject-centred in their views of education and those who wish to eliminate it are more student-centred in their views. In general, teachers thought that teaching was easier in ability-grouped classes. This US-based project also found that parents are important influences on decisions about ability grouping.

Difficulties of mixed-ability teaching

A different perspective on mixed-ability teaching is given by Reid *et al* (1981). In a survey of headteachers and teachers, they found that the headteachers had abandoned streaming for both ethical and practical reasons: they felt mixed-ability teaching would give the pupils a fresh start, and at the same time had experienced difficulties in allocating pupils to streamed groups. However, teaching within mixed-ability groups presented serious difficulties, to the extent that it is doubtful how far the grouping enabled teachers to direct instruction to pupils' needs; quotations from several headteachers are given to the effect that 'We have mixed-ability groups but we do not do mixed-ability teaching'. Difficulties were encountered in:

- formulating teaching objectives
- organising the classroom to give each pupil appropriate attention
- teachers' ability to meet the pressures of mixed-ability teaching
- the extent to which teachers wanted to do mixed-ability teaching
- the extent to which teachers wanted to work together
- finding time to prepare teachers.

Teachers claimed to see social advantages in mixed-ability classes, but Reid *et al* note their inability to be specific about these, and their unwillingness to explore this issue further. Disadvantages concerned increased workload, lack of resources, a perception that the more able pupils showed reduced motivation and the difficulty of meeting pupil needs effectively, especially when the spread of ability was very wide. Reid *et al* add that the teachers made little comment on average pupils, and wonder whether these, the majority, are overlooked and the range of their individual differences ignored.

Teacher behaviour was highlighted in a study by Rosenbaum (1976) (cited in Good and Marshall, 1984) carried out with high school pupils, which showed that the same teachers gave different kinds of attention to different classes, with less concern and effort going to those who were not in the stream aiming for college entrance. This was described as 'prima facie evidence that the academic needs of the low-track pupils were simply not being met in low-track classes'.

Gregory (1984) identified the following problems with streaming and mixed-ability teaching:

- low teacher expectation is followed by poor pupil progress (Winn and Wilson, 1983, citing Tuckman and Bierman, 1971)
- teacher behaviours and school organisation respond differentially to different ability groups (Winn and Wilson, 1983), for example, upper ability groups received more teacher time, more praise, less direction and criticism in a USA secondary school; lower ability groups had fewer opportunities to respond; teachers of slow learning groups stressed basic skills, facts and drill, used

unimaginative teaching approaches (one study only); the lower group had access to fewer science materials, poorer library facilities, less competent teachers

- mixed-ability teaching involves more work for the teacher as the burden of preparation is daunting (Wilcox, 1961; Davies, 1975; Kelly, 1975)

- many teachers are not trained to do mixed-ability teaching (Collier, 1982)

- bright pupils in mixed-ability classes are not being stretched academically (Wragg, 1984; HMI, 1978): in fact these teams experienced great difficulty in finding any mixed-ability teaching and reported that less able children were not being catered for

- even teachers considered effective in handling mixed-ability classes frequently used whole-class teaching, made no provision for the least able, had discipline problems, streamed classes into ability groups and gave no evidence of any kind of selective approach to pupils of differing abilities (Kerry, 1982a, 1982b).

Gregory's conclusion with regard to the difficulties associated with streaming (or setting) and mixed-ability grouping is that 'the most pervasive problem with setting or streaming probably is the risk of lowered teacher expectation for the lower ability groups. With mixed-ability there is no conclusive evidence that such grouping enhances social interactions and its major problem is the need for huge supplementary material to realise the aims of individualised instruction. Many teachers, finding this a problem, resort to whole-class teaching which is often an inappropriate teaching method with mixed-ability classes'.

Simpson and Ure (1993) drew attention to lack of differentiation in tasks set to pupils in mixed-ability classes in early secondary classes in Scotland. From interviews with pupils about the difficulty of their work, the researchers found considerable evidence that all pupils found their work too easy. This highlights the lack of appropriately differentiated tasks in mixed-ability teaching.

Problems of creating ability groups
The imprecise and often biased allocation of pupils to ability groups has been pointed out by Neave (1975) and Winn and Wilson (1983).

Oakes (1995) provides an illustration of some of the difficulties in ensuring a fair and educationally-valuable allocation of pupils to streams, which had been one of the factors motivating the headteachers in the Reid study to change to mixed-ability groupings. In a study of the unequal treatment of African-American and Latino children in two school districts in the USA, she found that:

- The criteria used to assign pupils to particular tracks were neither clearly specified nor consistently applied (to the disadvantage of non-white pupils)
  - the ability groups did not narrow the range of ability
  - teacher judgements about placement were often subjective and based on judgement about behaviour, personality and attitudes
  - parents' wishes about the stream in which their children should be placed were met.
- Classes that were supposed to be for pupils at a particular ability level actually contained pupils who spanned a very wide range of measured ability, ie they were not homogeneous
  - pupils with the same test scores were not necessarily placed in similar streams; this was always to the disadvantage of African-American and Latino pupils.
- Low streams provided less learning opportunity
  - teachers expected less of these pupils
  - teachers gave them less exposure to curriculum and teaching in essential knowledge and skills
  - they had less access to a range of resources and opportunities (eg highly qualified teachers; classroom environments conducive to learning; opportunities to earn grade points; courses to qualify them for college entrance and a wide range of adult careers).
- Low streams were associated with low achievement
  - the difference in achievement scores between white and other pupils in first grade did not diminish in higher grades, they had increased by eleventh grade. Oakes comments that '[these] grouping practices... did not serve a remedial function for minority students... Students who were placed in lower-level courses... consistently demonstrate lesser gains in achievement over time than their peers placed in high-level courses... [and]

whether students began with relatively high or relatively low achievement, those who were placed in lower-level courses showed lesser gains over time than similarly situated students who were placed in higher-level courses.'

Although Oakes focuses on her finding that racial discrimination was operating in the streaming practices of the schools in the study (she used the evidence as expert witness in litigation between the school districts and the court), the study seems to provide evidence of major weaknesses in streaming: the difficulty of allocating pupils to grades in a way that will ensure true homogeneity of ability, and differences in teacher expectations and behaviour with different streams and social classes.

A study by Balow (1964) additionally illustrates that factors other than test scores contribute to placement decisions. Using maths tests different from those used for group placement, Balow found that there was enormous overlap between pupils in supposedly homogeneous seventh grade mathematics classes.

Cahan and Linchevski (1996) demonstrated that ability grouping increases the gap between pupils at different levels. Their studies in schools in Israel, to which further reference is made later (pp45, 50) concluded that pupils with similar initial scores in mathematics, when placed in different ability groups, diverged in attainment. Those assigned to the upper group gained more than those assigned to the lower group and this gap increased year by year. In other words, sets became a self-fulfilling prophecy.

Boaler (1997a, 1997b) reported that many pupils did not feel that they had been put into the right sets. Boys, particularly, considered that they were judged by their behaviour rather than their subject ability. Tomlinson's work provides supporting evidence of such discrimination. Troyna (1991), in case-study work in a multiracial comprehensive secondary school, drew attention to the longer-term effects of placement in sets at the point of entry to secondary school. This early placement, he argued, disadvantaged Asian pupils in their later GCSE results. Moreover, the claim that pupils can readily transfer between streams and sets is not supported by evidence. Devine (1993) reported that such transfer was less than expected and less than was required.

Ability grouping in subject-specific research
Perceptions of different subjects

As noted above, Slavin (1990) makes no major distinction between streaming and setting, stating that there were no differences in the outcomes of different forms of ability grouping. Slavin also makes the point that there was no discernible pattern of findings with respect to different subjects, except that some studies (Marascuilo and McSweeney, 1972; Fowlkes, 1931) 'found relatively strong effects favouring heterogeneous grouping in social studies'. Marascuilo and McSweeney found that, over a two-year period, pupils in the top social studies classes gained slightly more than similar pupils in mixed-ability classes, but across seven multi-year correlational studies up to five years in length, not one found a clear pattern of differential effects. Other research (Peterson, 1966; Martin, 1927 and Postlethwaite and Denton, 1978) found either no difference or only slight effects in the same direction. Slavin adds that this is not enough evidence to point conclusively to a positive effect of heterogeneous grouping in social studies, but stresses that the studies which found differences in that direction were of particularly high quality.

The research carried out by Reid *et al* (1981), who worked with almost 500 teachers almost all of whom were 'substantially involved with mixed-ability classes', picked up the point of the suitability of different subjects to different forms of class organisation. They found that teachers viewed some subjects as suitable and others unsuitable for mixed-ability grouping. A major factor in this seemed to be the structure of the subject: if it required pupils to work through a body of knowledge in logical sequence, the problems of teaching mixed-ability groups were thought insuperable. In contrast, teaching mixed-ability groups was made easier when the subject permitted division into a number of relatively independent themes or topics. Hence humanities subjects were thought suitable for mixed-ability groups while modern languages and mathematics were not.

A further main factor was the teacher's classroom role: if the teacher was seen as the central or major resource, fewer possibilities for mixed-ability grouping were seen. Reid *et al* comment: 'The teaching of modern languages, where class teaching was used extensively, illustrates this point well; in no other subject did almost one-third of the staff employ class teaching as the dominant organisational mode'. Modern linguists were the least likely to see advantages in mixed-ability grouping, particularly if the teacher was widely viewed as the main resource.

Other factors which teachers thought determined the suitability or otherwise of a subject for mixed-ability teaching were the extent to which pupils needed familiarity with technical vocabulary, were subjected to examination pressures, and were expected to produce academic outcomes. The stronger these needs, the less suited the subject was thought to be.

Reid *et al* found a widespread use of whole-class teaching. For some of the teachers this was the dominant teaching mode, but many used it as one of a battery of teaching strategies. The researchers acknowledge it to be important that teachers can select the most effective strategy for the task in hand, and that there will be occasions when this is whole-class teaching, but they add, 'to attempt to teach a heterogeneous group of pupils in this way in inappropriate circumstances can present formidable problems'. (These were noted earlier on p38.) The conclusion from their research is that 'there are no certain outcomes, either positive or negative, which can be assumed to follow inevitably from mixed-ability grouping or, probably, from any other form of organisation'.

Mathematics

Although the two comprehensive reviews by Slavin (1987 and 1990) showed no differences in achievement for any groups or for any subjects between streamed and mixed-ability groups, it is worth looking particularly at studies in mathematics and science since in these subjects there is assumed to be a rationale for setting. As Reid's study indicates, teachers perceive mathematics as a strongly hierarchical subject where it would be difficult to cover the wide range of ability in an age group using differentiated materials in mixed-ability classes. Research comparing setting and mixed-ability teaching in this subject might, therefore, be expected to yield results showing advantages of setting if there were any to be found.

Two recent studies are important because they provide evidence about the effect of grouping on the performance of individual pupils as well as statistical evidence across groups. These were carried out in mathematics and although the quantitative and qualitative information relates to fourth and fifth year pupils of secondary school, there are undoubtedly implications for classes in the first two years of the secondary school.

Linchevski conducted four longitudinal studies relating to mathematical attainment and pupil grouping in Israel (Linchevski, 1995a, 1995b). In one of the studies Linchevski compared the eventual attainment of pupils in twelve setted schools with their expected attainment, based upon entry scores. This showed that ability grouping had no effect on attainment in ten of the schools and a small negative effect in the other two. A second study examined the thinking and performance of similar-ability pupils who were at the border of different ability bands and assigned to different groups. This showed that the pupils of similar ability assigned to different groups varied in attainment, with the pupils assigned to higher groups attaining more than pupils of a similar ability assigned to lower groups. Linchevski concluded from this that 'the achievements of students close to the cut off points are largely dependent on their being arbitrarily assigned to a lower or higher group level' (Linchevski, 1995a, p11). Another of her studies compared the achievements of two groups of pupils at the same school assigned either to setted or mixed-ability groups. This showed that the average scores of the most able pupils placed in setted groups were slightly, but not significantly, higher than the able pupils placed in mixed-ability groups. However, the scores of pupils in the two lower setted groups were significantly lower than similar-ability pupils in the mixed-ability classes. Linchevski found that low-ability pupils in the mixed-ability classes coped well with tests because they were used to high demands and expectations. Boaler (1997a) quotes other studies in mathematics which have found differences in achievement between homogeneous and heterogeneous groupings that replicate Linchevski's finding with some small, statistically insignificant increases for pupils in high-ability groups, gained at the expense of large, statistically significant losses for pupils in low-ability groups (Hoffer, 1992; Kerchkoff, 1986).

In a recent UK research study Boaler (1997b, 1997c,) combined aspects of the UK and US studies reported by performing an in-depth study of pupils over a long period of time that focused upon pupils' attainment in addition to their beliefs and values. The research included case studies of two year groups (of over 100 pupils) in two schools. In one school, mathematics was taught in a mixed-ability environment, in the other in a highly differentiated, setted environment. The pupils were matched in terms of their ability, sex, ethnicity and socio-economic status at the start of the research. They were then observed in lessons, interviewed and assessed at regular intervals during the three-year period. This research differed from other studies because it considered the attainment of pupils taught in setted and mixed-ability groups, alongside the pupils' perceptions of positive and negative learning experiences in the different situations. It produced the following results:

- In the mixed-ability school, the pupils attained higher GCSE grades and significantly more A-G passes (88% of the cohort compared with 71%), despite the fact that pupils were of the same ability in both schools at the start of their schooling, measured on national, standardised tests.

- In the school using setting, the biggest determining factor upon achievement at GCSE was social class, which was more important than an ability measure taken on entry to the school. In the mixed-ability school, social class was not linked to achievement.

- The effects of setting disadvantaged a significant proportion of top-set pupils. A number of pupils, taught by different teachers, were negatively affected by the pace, pressure and expectations formed within top-set environments in years nine to eleven. This was shown to particularly disadvantage the highest ability girls who had previously been very successful in mixed-ability settings in years seven and eight (first two years of secondary).

- In interviews, the pupils reported that working at the pace of the class (as is common practice in setted classes) negatively affected their understanding compared with working at their own pace. This was because, for much of the time, they were forced to work at a pace that was either too fast (which inhibited their understanding and created anxiety) or too slow (which led to disaffection and under-achievement). When they worked at their 'own pace' in mixed-ability classes the pupils reported a greater depth of understanding.

- In the school using setting, social class influenced setting decisions resulting in disproportionate numbers of working class pupils being allocated to low sets.

- The limits placed upon the achievement of pupils in set two downwards, caused many pupils to become disillusioned and demotivated: they believed that they could have achieved more if they had been allowed to, and this negatively affected their pre-disposition towards work.

On the basis of her research, Boaler (1993) suggests that the reason why setting is ineffective is that teachers assume that they have a homogeneous group, and that therefore there is no need to allow for differences in pace and other individual differences in learning. In reality, however, individual differences do exist and it is just as necessary to cater for them as in mixed-ability groups. In the latter, teachers do not make the assumption that all the pupils are the same and use methods and materials that allow pupils to work at their own pace.

The pace of the work was the focus of discontent in setted classes, both from those who thought it too slow and those who could not keep up, and, in fact, then gave up. Indeed, one aspect of Boaler's work was that she uncovered a serious problem for some pupils in the top sets, particularly girls. She quotes two girls who were in the top set as making the following comments in interview: 'You're expected to know everything, even if you're not sure about things', 'You're pushed too hard', 'He expects you to work all the time at a high level', 'It makes me do less work, they expect too much of me and I can't give it so I just give up'. These two girls had the highest NFER score on entering the secondary school but attained grade E in their GCSE examinations.

Meanwhile, the pupils in the lower sets were aware that their sights were restricted by their position; they knew that whatever they did they would not obtain more than a Grade C or D in maths. What all pupils wanted, however, in all sets, was to work at their own pace. When this was possible, as in the school where mixed-ability was practised and pupils were allowed more personal choice in how they worked, their GCSE results correlated more highly with their NFER mathematics score on entering school than was the case for the pupils in the school using setting. Boaler suggests that this means that setting introduced influences on learning unrelated to pupils' ability in mathematics. This suggestion was supported by an analysis of variance which showed that, in the mixed-ability school, initial mathematical ability was the only factor having a significant impact on GCSE achievement, whilst in the setted school the only factor so related was social class.

Science

Turning to science, a study of streamed and mixed-ability classes reported by Hacker, Rowe and Evans (1991, 1992) is important because it provides classroom observation data about the behaviours of teachers and pupils in different groupings. The observations were carried out in three schools where a change from streamed to mixed-ability classes was planned. Prior to the introduction of the change, lessons taught to 14-year olds by nine science teachers in the three schools were observed. At that time pupils were streamed into two bands by ability in science. For each teacher two classes were selected, one from the high ability band and one from the low ability band, and the teacher was observed teaching six lessons to each class. Six pupils were observed in each class. Their non-verbal interactions were recorded on videotape by a fixed wide-angle lens camera and their verbal interactions were recorded by radio microphones. A microphone was worn by the teacher. The analysis of the observations, using the Science Lesson Analysis System (SLAS), focused on the forms of interaction (for example, types of verbal and non-verbal interactions) and the functions of the interactions (eg acquiring knowledge, identifying problems, interpreting observations).

Findings from the high- and low-ability classes taught by the same teacher showed little difference in the frequency of interactions. However, there were quite large differences in the forms and functions of the interactions: 'Lessons taught to high-ability classes were characterised by more independent learning and development of a broad range of intellectual abilities, whereas lessons taught to low-ability classes were characterised in terms of greater teacher direction, and more emphasis being placed upon a relatively narrow range of lower-order informational behaviours' (Hacker, Rowe and

Evans, 1992). The difference was particularly marked in periods of practical work.

One year after the organisational change had been made in the schools, the data-gathering procedures were repeated using the same teachers. Again six pupils in each class were targets for observation, chosen equally from pupils who would have been allocated to the high- and low-ability bands in the former system. The types of interactions were then compared for high- and low-ability pupils taught in homogeneous and heterogeneous classes.

The findings showed very few differences in the interactions of low-ability pupils but in the case of the high-ability groups there were marked changes, such that the researchers concluded: 'indeed, mixed-ability classes appear to be treated as though they were low-ability streams'. They also noted that there was little evidence in the mixed-ability classes of true individualised teaching and 'it is difficult to escape the conclusion that the teacher tended to teach to the middle of the ability range in mixed-ability classes rather than individualising activities'. In their view, this would account for the poorer performance of able pupils when taught in mixed-ability classes than when taught in ability streams or sets.

However, the study also revealed that there was a large gap between what teachers thought they were providing for pupils and what was actually observed. The researchers commented: 'whereas all the participating teachers professed to having adopted individualised approaches, classroom observations revealed dissonance between teacher perceptions and classroom practice, with less than ten per cent of class time being allocated to true, individualised activities... more commonly 'individualised' teaching merely involved pupils working at their own pace on structured worksheets, with all pupils studying the same topic'. Thus, again, as in so many studies, organisational change was confounded with treatment of pupils and with a retention of teaching style more appropriate to the teaching of homogeneous groups.

A study by Taylor (1993), although it was carried out with fourth year secondary school pupils, provides evidence that setting in the first and second years reinforces social divisions between high and low achievers and sends damaging messages to pupils placed in the lower sets, thus confirming earlier findings by Hargreaves (1967). Examining the allocation to sets of 80 fourth year pupils in a comprehensive school in England, Taylor found that pupils from higher income areas tended to appear in the top three sets and those from poorer backgrounds in the four lowest sets. Taylor comments that 'for children from poorer backgrounds, who may already have low self-esteem, being put into set six or seven so early in their school career can only serve to reduce their self-esteem further'. He adds that the polarising effect 'did not have major implications for behaviour early on, but by the fourth and fifth years many pupils had very obviously opted out and were channelling their energy into disruptive behaviour'. Interviews with fourth year boys, in the same low set for most subjects, showed that for them 'setting is effectively streaming'. They felt there was no point in working hard because they weren't good enough to get into the higher sets; that making progress within the set was hard because other boys were disruptive and the teacher spent a lot of time controlling them rather than teaching those who wanted to work, and that the teachers were to blame for not controlling poor behaviour better. Furthermore, they disliked the pupils in the top sets.

English

Gamoran *et al* (1995) reported an extensive study of tracking in English in 92 eighth and ninth grade classes in 18 US schools. Their study is important because it was designed to throw light on what supports and what impedes pupils in different ability classes and to help understanding of why the gap between lower and higher sets or streams widens over time. (See Cahan and Linchevski, cited on p42).

Gamoran *et al* examined the backgrounds of pupils and found the pattern of high correlation of ability group with socio-economic status, race and ethnicity that has been well established in other studies and reviewed by Oakes, Gamoran and Page (1992). Through classroom observation and interview techniques, they obtained quantitative measures of teacher-student interaction. These were related to 'participation' (pupils being on-task), 'coherence' (teachers linking new material to previous lessons), 'uptake' (teachers eliciting and using pupils' responses), teachers' questioning (asking 'real' questions as opposed to ones where they are looking for particular answers), and discussion (the free exchange of opinions). The researchers also noted the percentage of their reading and writing tasks that the pupils completed. Learning outcomes were measured by a year-end test of 'literature achievement' tailored to the particular materials covered in each class during the year.

The results showed that, for all ability groups, high achievement was strongly correlated with completing their reading and writing tasks, with more 'uptake' and 'coherence' in the teaching. For the lower and medium ability groups, off-task behaviour was associated with lower achievement, but this was not the case for the higher-level groups. More 'real' questioning was associated with high achievement for the most able, but not for the medium and least able. Similarly, discussion promoted achievement in higher-level groups but not in others. In their discussion, Gamoran *et al* indicate that the types of questions and discussion in the lower ability classes may have been responsible for the lack of effect in improving performance and they recommend that:

> To the extent that ability grouping continues to be used, our results suggest that achievement inequality could be reduced by raising the calibre of both instructional content and instructional discourse in regular and remedial classes. In addition, the findings indicate that high-quality instructional discourse – characterised by student participation, coherence, discussion, authenticity, and uptake – can improve student learning when it occurs in the context of substantive academic content. The data fail to support our speculation that authentic discourse and discussion are especially beneficial to academically at-risk students – perhaps not because such instruction is ineffective, but because little of this type of instruction occurred in low-ability classes studying literature – and this remains, in our view, an open question.
>
> (Gamoran *et al*, 1995, p708)

Within-class grouping

In his 1990 review, Slavin himself commented that there were relatively few studies of the effect of within-class grouping in high schools. Among them was that of Campbell (1965) who compared ability maths groups with mixed-ability maths groups, and found no achievement differences. Harrah (1956), working with grades seven to nine, found ability grouping to be no more successful than other grouping methods. Referring to his own earlier review (1987) Slavin notes that these findings conflict with those of studies in upper primary schools (elementary grades) which tend to support the use of ability groups for mathematics. Chismar (1971) compared a cross-grade grouping in reading with a within-class group in reading and found significantly positive effects in grades four and seven but not in five, six and eight.

The later meta-analysis by Lou *et al* (1996) was devoted to studies of within-class grouping. Looking across 51 studies involving pupils from grade one to post-secondary, from which 103 independent effects were extracted, they compared the effects of within-class grouping with no grouping. Effects were greatest for late elementary grades and rather less, but still significant, for secondary grades. There were significant effects at all class sizes, but these were greatest for large classes (35 or more).

An analysis of 21 studies where pupils' attitudes were compared in grouped and ungrouped classes found that within-class grouping was positively related to pupil attitudes overall and particularly to attitudes towards the subject matter. Pupils in grouped classes were also found to have significantly higher self-concepts than those in ungrouped classes. When ability-based groups were compared with mixed ability groups, those in ability groups achieved at a slightly higher level than those in mixed ability groups, with pupils of medium ability gaining most. However it is important to point out that the effects due to differences in treatment wiped out any differences due to grouping; small groups using cooperative learning in a task with a combined outcome achieved far more than small groups not working on collaborative tasks. Similarly, experiential learning was associated with greater achievement than within-class grouping (Lou *et al*, 1996, p443).

Summary

- Streaming and setting – and sometimes a combination of both – were common in secondary schools up to the 1960s; as in primary schools, the change to mixed-ability grouping, at least in the first two secondary years, was in reaction to evidence of its socially divisive consequences.

- Ability grouping in sets or streams has been found to have no overall effect on achievement, compared with mixed ability grouping; advantages for high ability pupils have been found where advanced curriculum materials have been used.

- Creating sets is often influenced by factors other than pupil ability; once in a set, the gap in achievement between lower and higher attainers widens and there is little transfer between sets.

- Early allocation to sets or streams is discouraging for the lower attaining pupils and reinforces social divisions.

- Mixed-ability teaching makes great demands on teachers in terms of workload.

- Many mixed-ability classes are not taught in a way that caters for mixed ability; observation studies indicate that mixed-ability classes are often taught as if they were of the same ability and all of lower than average ability.

- Even within sets, there is a considerable range in pace of learning and it is necessary to cater for individual differences; in particular, it has been shown that high-ability girls dislike working under pressure.

- In mathematics, ability grouping can lead to better achievement for all providing that the teaching materials are differentiated.

- Inequalities in the type of pupil-teacher interaction between setted or streamed classes results in the widening of the gap between the higher and lower achieving classes.

4

Discussion and Conclusions

Ability grouping is used to reduce the diversity among pupils who are taught together. The rationale for forming groups by attainment is that teachers can then deal with different groups in different ways. When we come to consider the evidence of whether this 'works' in terms of enabling more learning by all the pupils, regardless of ability, the research results are equivocal. Indeed, reviewing studies on the effects of grouping pupils by ability could easily generate cynicism about educational research. There is something to please everyone – some studies lend support to grouping by ability, some point in the opposite direction, and many show that there is little difference that can be ascribed only to the type of grouping. The reason for so much ambiguity is that this is a very difficult area for research. Studies of setting or streaming generally involve comparison of classes containing a full range of ability with those in which pupils are more similar in ability. However the relative performance of pupils is affected by many variables other than the mix of ability, for example, class size, ability range, teaching methods and materials, the degree of differentiation, the attitude of the teacher towards mixed-ability teaching and the curriculum content.

Moreover, there are difficulties in forming groups in a way that does not reinforce the social divisions found outside the school, for it is undeniable that ability-group status is correlated with socio-economic status. A further problem is caused by a general lack of knowledge about the best way to treat different ability groups. As Gamoran *et al* (1995) point out: 'There is little consensus about what constitutes the best teaching methods, so it is difficult for educators to know precisely how to vary their teaching for different groups' (p689).

Research studies vary considerably in the attention they give to the many factors which can influence pupils' achievement over and above any impact of ability or mixed-ability grouping. We have used the concept of 'best evidence synthesis' to sift through the research evidence and use what is most reliable. What, then, can we say?

Primary

The research at primary / elementary level provides no evidence that achievement of pupils is raised either by streaming or setting within the school. In a country such as Scotland, with predominantly small schools, the opportunities for forming homogeneous ability classes are limited in any case; but even if this were not so, the research points to what happens within the class as being the important matter, and not how classes are constituted. The social disadvantage pointed to by research in the US, where elementary schools are often as large as secondaries, indicates that since there are no advantages of academic achievement to be had from streaming, it is not a policy to be advocated. The case against setting or 'regrouping' is rather less clear cut since there is some evidence of benefit in mathematics for the more able. However, even this is qualified in terms of being dependent on these pupils having the pace and materials for instruction adapted to their needs: 'Simply regrouping without extensively adapting materials, or regrouping in all academic subjects, is ineffective' (Slavin, 1987, p311).

Nevertheless, as the recent survey in England by Lee and Croll (1995) shows, some headteachers support the principle of streaming. This may be because of a false assumption that the research evidence is different from what is actually the case, or because of the difficulties teachers have with mixed-ability classes, particularly when they are increasing in size. Bennett (1996) reported over 9,000 pupils in classes of over 40, whilst more recent figures indicate that in 1996 41% of primary pupils in Britain were in classes of over 30 children. This focuses attention on the over-riding factor of what is happening inside the classes.

The report of the rapid increase in setting in primary schools in England (OfSTED, 1998), was accompanied by caveats that adopting setting did not automatically bring advantages in terms of pupil achievements. The view of the inspectors was that the teachers who were taking 'full advantage of setting' were those who emphasised whole-class interactive teaching, who had realistic but challenging expectations for their pupils, and who used lesson time effectively. Indeed, their teaching displayed all the characteristics of 'direct teaching' urged by HM Inspectors of Schools in Scotland (SOEID, 1996) and quoted on p17. Although not underpinned by hard evidence, the English inspectors' observations support the view that it is these characteristics of teaching that improve achievement. Setting is an aid and, in some cases, a stimulus to such teaching.

It is rather too early for systematic research to have followed the rise in popularity of setting in the 1990s, but there is anecdotal evidence that gives room for optimism that some of the lessons from earlier studies of setting have been learned. Where this is the case, schools are introducing setting in a way that maximises its advantages and minimises its disadvantages. For example, rotating teachers around sets ensures that all have the opportunity to teach across the ability range and that any weakness in teaching is not disadvantaging lower attainers. In this way teachers do not lose contact with the pupils in their class for the setted subject and they are all aware of how learning experiences are differentiated according to ability. Such rotation demands joint planning of teaching and assists discussion of the learning of individual pupils. This increases the likelihood of pupils being moved to a more appropriate set according to progress.

In such conditions it has been observed that the separation of pupils by ability can have advantages for the lower attainers whose work is not constantly open to comparison with the high flyers and who can use concrete aids without being thought 'babyish'. We emphasise, however, that these anecdotal observations, although based on experience, are not outcomes of systematic research and do not provide any evidence for judging any impact on achievement.

The strongest evidence for the effect of ability grouping on achievement was in relation to within-class ability groups for mathematics. Pupils of all abilities gained from this as compared with whole-class teaching. Grouping by ability makes it easier for the teacher to provide appropriate learning challenges and support for each child. Some teachers manage to do this when pupils are grouped by friendship and not ability. Others manage more effectively in ability groups. What the research shows is that it is this provision of differentiated learning experiences which is important; ability grouping is one way of achieving it.

Within-class grouping for at least some of the time is almost universal. When this grouping is heterogeneous and used simply to reduce the number of pupils the teacher interacts with at any one time, in theory, the differences in ability can be catered for at the individual level. When the grouping is homogeneous, the research shows that the teacher interacts differently with the more and the less able pupils. This can be to the detriment of the less able, as the summary of research findings (p30) has shown. The less able often have less well-developed skills for working in groups, they tend to interrupt each other, work on tasks that are less stimulating than those of more able groups, and receive less 'quality' attention from the teacher. Thus, within-class ability grouping introduces some of the social effects of streaming, albeit with a less strong impact.

The message that emerges is that within-class ability grouping is the only form of ability-group found to have advantages for pupils' achievement levels. This has been shown only in maths; there is an absence of research in other areas. However, ability grouping has potential disadvantages of which teachers should be aware. To avoid the detrimental effects it would appear advisable to use such grouping as little as possible and at other times to ensure that pupils have the benefits of working with others both more and less able than themselves.

Secondary

In relation to setting and streaming in the secondary school, the research findings mirror those of primary school research. There is no consistent and reliable evidence of positive effects of setting and streaming in any subjects, or for pupils of particular ability levels. Indeed, the clearest finding meeting the best-evidence criterion is that heterogeneous groups are an advantage in social subjects. Otherwise, the findings are contradictory, the differences arising from methodological difficulties related to this area of work, such as the basis on which ability groups are created, the extent to which the teaching methods used are appropriate to heterogeneous or homogeneous groups, and the attitudes of the teachers.

When ability groups are formed by setting or streaming, their disadvantages are well documented: reinforced social-class divisions; increased likelihood of delinquent behaviour in the later school years; lowered teacher expectations of the less able; bias and inconsistency in allocating pupils to ability groups; anxiety for pupils struggling to keep up with the pace of the class. This makes ability grouping hard to defend; yet mixed-ability grouping has its own drawbacks.

As with the primary school evidence, what seems to be of critical importance is what takes place inside classrooms. The evidence suggests that mixed-ability classes are hard to manage and that teachers aim lessons at the middle of the ability range when working with them; sometimes, indeed, treating mixed-ability groups as though they were low-ability streams. It is revealing that, as the UK study by Reid *et al* (1981) shows, even teachers with substantial experience of working with mixed-ability classes frequently use whole-class teaching methods which are inappropriate to mixed-ability groupings. Furthermore, as suggested by Hacker, Rowe and Evans (1991, 1992), although teachers consider themselves to be individualising work, observation of their lessons does not bear out this belief.

It is notable that unlike the research done in primary schools, that at secondary level finds no benefit in within-class ability groups. This may simply stem from the paucity of research on such groupings in secondary schools. It may, however, be related to the point made above: that even when teachers believe they are catering for pupil differences, in fact they are not; and it may also be relevant that although some studies found slight evidence of benefit in ability groups, this was so only when more advanced curriculum materials were used for these pupils. Unless secondary school teachers are able, in practice, to adapt the curriculum and their teaching methods to the demands that individual pupils' needs make, it may make little difference to pupils' achievement how classes are grouped.

In the early years of secondary school in Scotland there is a curriculum common to all pupils, and the challenge to the teacher is to provide the optimum learning opportunities for all pupils whilst covering this ground. This means that there has to be some way of catering for their individual needs. The research provides no support for separating pupils according to ability as a solution to this problem. Indeed, it shows that for many, ability grouping reduces both their motivation and the quality of the education they are offered. The alternatives are to adjust the content, pace and support to suit individual needs. Here the research evidence is not very helpful since it does not identify the means by which 'individualisation' is achieved, although this term is frequently used in the discussion. In many cases it appears to mean pupils working through the same material 'at their own pace'; that is, on their own, with little help from their peers or their teacher. Recently this approach has been criticised, particularly in mathematics, where it is most prevalent.

Perhaps the secondary school would benefit from adopting, in its first two years, the practice that the research shows to be the most effective way of helping pupils' mathematics achievement in the primary school; that is, within-class grouping. This would enable pupils to have more interaction with the teacher and support from peers. The lack of research on this matter in secondary schools suggests that this is a significant gap that needs to be filled. Flexible within-class grouping could ensure that, where it is appropriate to work in ability groups, these are formed on the basis of achievement in a particular curriculum area and not on some basis of 'general ability', which is often mixed with social background.

Other ways of raising standards of achievement

The conclusion that appears as the most prominent theme through the research, however, is that what is important in determining achievement is that the challenge and support given to learners meet their needs. Reducing the range of ability in groups may make this easier in some subjects but giving each pupil an appropriate challenge will always be necessary whatever the grouping. By the same token the formation of ability groups can often have the effect of reducing learning opportunities, either through lowering the motivation of the learners or through lowering the quality of the experiences they are given. In any event, as Hallam and Toutounji (1996) pointed out from their review of research, ability grouping is only one of a number of factors that relate to school effectiveness.

Since the drive to re-introduce setting emerges from the aim of raising standards, it is relevant to point out that in studies where difference between pupils taught in ability groups and in mixed ability settings were found, there were concomitant factors that could well have explained the difference. For example, Askew and Wiliam (1995) noted in their review of research in mathematics the factors listed below as being associated with improvements in performance, in addition to small positive effects due to grouping by attainment:

- linking practical tasks to abstract mathematics
- taking steps to elicit and address pupils' mathematical misconceptions
- careful choice of examples
- effective use of questions
- using praise effectively
- assessing progress regularly and using this to adapt learning experiences
- use of calculators in learning
- use of computers in learning
- using a wide range of problem-solving situations
- cooperative group work.

Similarly, Medwell *et al* (1998) identified, for the Teacher Training Agency, characteristics of the beliefs and practices of effective teachers of literacy. Many of these features are included in the notion of 'direct teaching' as it is broadly interpreted (p17). There is also much overlap with the concept of 'formative assessment' whose effect on attainment was the subject of an extensive research review by Black and Wiliam (1988). As a result of reviewing over 250 studies, Black and Wiliam revealed evidence that changes in assessment procedures are effective in raising levels of achievement. The key features of assessment that would accomplish this were identified as:

- the provision of effective feedback to pupils
- the active involvement of pupils in their own learning
- adjusting teaching to take account of the results of assessment

- a recognition of the profound influence of assessment on the motivation and self-esteem of pupil
- the need for pupils to be able to assess themselves and understand how to improve their achievement.

These features are at the heart of pupil-teacher interaction and the evidence is that, when implemented, they have a greater effect on achievement in terms of effect sizes than that reported for changes in class organisation. However some forms of class organisation are more likely than others to facilitate the implementation of these features of effective teaching and this may vary among teachers and curriculum subjects. This suggests that the particular form of class organisation should be selected on the basis of the degree to which it facilitates opportunities for teaching that combine the key features of direct teaching and those promoting effective use of assessment to determine pupils' next steps in learning.

References

indicates a study considered in depth in this review.

*Alexander, R.J. (1991) *Primary Education in Leeds.* Leeds University.

Arlin, M. (1979) Teacher transitions can disrupt time flow in classrooms. *American Educational Research Journal*, 16, 42–56.

Askew, M. & Wiliam, D. (1995) *Recent Research in Mathematics Education 5–16.* London: OfSTED.

Balow, I.H. (1964) The effects of 'homogeneous' grouping in seventh grade arithmetic. *Arithmetic Teacher*, 12, 186–191.

Balow, I.H. & Ruddell, A.K. (1963) The effects of three types of grouping on achievement. *California Journal of Educational Research*, 14, 108–117.

*Barker–Lunn, J.C. (1970) *Streaming in the Primary School.* Slough: National Foundation for Educational Research in England & Wales.

Bealing, D. (1972) The organisation of junior school classrooms. *Educational Research*, 14 (3) 231–5.

Becker, W.C. (1977) Teaching reading and language to the disadvantaged – what we have learnt from field research. *Harvard Education Review*, 47, 518–543.

Begle, E.G. (1975) *Ability grouping for mathematical instruction: a review of the empirical literature.* Stamford University Mathematics Education Study Group (ERIC Document ED116938).

*Bennett, N. *et al* (1976) *Teaching Styles and Pupil Progress.* Open Books.

*Bennett, N. (1996) Class size in primary schools: perceptions of head teachers, chairs of governors, teachers and parents. *British Educational Research Journal*, 22 (1), 33–56.

Bereiter, C. (1972) Schools without education. *Harvard Educational Review*, 42 (3), 390–413.

Berkun, M.M., Swanson, L.W. & Sawyer, D.M. (1966) An experiment on homogeneous grouping for reading in elementary classes. *Journal of Educational Research*, 59, 413–414.

Black, P.J. & Wiliam, D. (1998) Assessment and classroom learning. *Assessment in Education*, 5 (1) 7–74.

Blair, T. (1996) *Comprehensive schools: a new vision,* Speech by Rt. Hon. Tony Blair at Didcot Girls' School, Oxfordshire, June 7 (Labour Party press release).

Boaler, J. (1993) Encouraging the transfer of 'school' mathematics to the 'real world' through the interaction of process and contents, context and culture. *Educational Studies in Mathematics*, 25 (4), 341–373.

*Boaler, J. (1997a) When even the winners are losers: evaluating the experiences of 'top set' students. *Journal of Curriculum Studies*, 29 (2), 165–182.

*Boaler, J. (1997b) *Experiencing School Mathematics: Teaching Styles, Sex and Setting*. Buckingham: Open University Press.

*Boaler, J. (1997c) Setting, social class and survival of the quickest. *British Educational Research Journal*, 23 (5), 575–596.

Borg, W.R. (1965) Ability grouping in the public schools: A field study. *Journal of Experimental Education*, 34, 1–97.

Breidenstine, A.G. (1936) The education of pupils in differentiated and undifferentiated groups. *Journal of Experimental Education*, 5, 91–135.

Bremer, N. (1958) First grade achievement under different plans of grouping. *Elementary English*, 35, 324–326.

Brophy, J.E. & Good, T.L. (1986) Teacher behaviour and student achievement. In: Wittrock, M.C. (Ed) *Handbook of Research on Teaching,* 3rd edition, 328–375. New York: Macmillan.

Bullock Committee of Enquiry into Reading and the Use of English (1975) *A Language for Life*. HMSO.

CACE (Central Advisory Committee on Education) (1967) *Children and their Primary Schools (Plowden Report)*. London: HMSO.

Cahan, S. & Linchevski, L. with Ygra, N. & Danziiger, I. (1996) The cumulative effect of ability grouping on mathematical achievement: a longitudinal perspective. *Studies in Educational Evaluation*, 22 (1), 29–40.

Calberg, C. & Kavale, K. (1980) The efficiency of special versus regular class placement for exceptional pupils: a meta–analysis. *Journal of Special Education*, 3.

Calfee, R.C. & Piontowski, D.C. (1987) Grouping for teaching. In: Dunkin, M.J. (Ed) *The International Encyclopaedia of Teaching and Teacher Education*, 225–232. Oxford: Pergamon Press.

Campbell, A.L. (1965) A comparison of the effectiveness of two methods of classroom organization for the teaching of arithmetic in junior high school. *Dissertation Abstracts International*, 26, 813–814 (University Microfilms No 65–6726).

Carnegie Council on Adolescent Development (1989) *Turning Points: Preparing American Youth for the 21st Century*. New York: Carnegie Corporation.

Cartwright, G.P. & McIntosh, D.K. (1972) Three approaches to grouping procedures for the education of disadvantaged primary school children. *Journal of Educational Research*, 65, 425–429.

Chismar, M.H. (1971) 'A study of the effectiveness of cross–level grouping of middle school underachievers for reading instruction'. Unpublished doctoral dissertation, Kent State University.

Collier, F. (1982) A retreat from mixed ability teaching. In: Sands, M. & Kerry, T. (Eds) *Mixed Ability Teaching.* Croom Helm.

Corson, D. (1987) *Oral Language Across the Curriculum.* Clevedon, Ohio: Multi-lingual Matters.

Cumbria County Council (1988) *Cumbria Oracy Project Principles and Practice.* Cumbria County Council Education Department.

Daniels, J.C. (1961) The effects of streaming in the primary school: comparison of streamed and unstreamed schools. *British Journal of Educational Psychology*, 31, 119–136.

Davie, R., Butler, N.R. & Goldstein, H. (1972) *From Birth to Seven.* Longman.

Davies, R.P. (1975) *Mixed Ability Grouping: Possibilities and Experiences in Secondary School.* Temple Smith.

Davis, O.L. & Tracy, N.H. (1963) Arithmetic achievement and instructional grouping. *Arithmetic Teacher*, 10, 12–17.

Department for Education (1993) *DfE News 16/93. Improving Primary Education – Pattern.* London: DfE.

DES (Department of Education and Science) (1979) *Aspects of Secondary Education in England: a survey by HM Inspectors of Schools.* HMSO.

Desforges, .C & Cockburn, A. (1986) *Understanding the Mathematics Teacher.* Falmer Press.

Devine, D. (1993) A study of reading ability groups: primary school children's experiences and views. *Irish Educational Studies*, 12, 134–42.

Dewar, J. (1964) Grouping for arithmetic instruction in sixth grade. *Elementary School Journal*, 63, 266–269.

Dougill, P. & Knott, R. (1988) *The Primary Language Book.* Milton Keynes: Open University Press.

Douglas, J.W.B. (1964) *The Home and the School.* McGibbon & Kee.

Douglas, J.W.B., Ross, J.M. & Simpson, H.R. (1968) *All Our Futures.* Peter Davies.

Eash, M J (1961) Grouping: What Have We Learned? *Educational Leadership*, 18, 429–434.

Edminston, R.W. & Benfer, J.G. (1949) The relationship between group achievement and range of abilities within groups. *Journal of Educational Research*, 42, 547–548.

Edwards, S. & Woodhead, N. (1996) Mathematics teaching in primary schools: whole class, group or individual teaching? *Primary Practice*, 6, 4–7.

Eilam, B. & Finegold, M. (1992) The heterogeneous class: a solution or just another problem? *Studies in Educational Evaluation*, 18 (2), 165–178.

Epstein, J.L. & MacIver, D.J. (1990) *Education in the Middle Grades: National Practices and Trends*. Columbus, Ohio: National Middle School Association.

Esposito, D. (1973) Homogeneous and heterogeneous ability grouping: principal findings and implications for evaluating and designing more effective educational environments. *Review of Educational Research*, 43, 163–179.

Essen, J., Fogelman, K. & Ghodsian, M. (1978) Long term changes in the school attainment of a national sample of children. *Educational Research*, 20, 143–151.

Evertson, C.M. (1989) Classroom organisation and management. In: Reynolds, M.C. (Ed) *Knowledge Base for the Beginner Teacher*. Oxford: Pergamon.

Ferri, E. (1971) *Streaming Two Years Later: A Follow–up of a Group of Pupils Who Attended Streamed and Non–streamed Junior Schools*. Slough: NFER.

Flair, M.D. (1964) The effect of grouping on achievement and attitudes towards learning of first grade pupils. *Dissertation Abstracts*, 25, 6430. (University Microfilms No 65–03, 259.)

Fogelman, K. (1975) Development correlates of family size. *British Journal of Social Work*, 5, 43–47.

Fogelman, K. & Goldstein H. (1976) Social factors associated with changes in educational attainment between 7 and 11 years of age. *Educational Studies*, 2, 95–109.

Fogelman, K., Essen, K. & Tibbenham, A. (1978) Ability grouping in secondary schools and attainment. *Educational Studies*, 4, 201–212.

Fowlkes, J.G. (1931) Homogeneous or heterogeneous groups – which? *The Nation's Schools*, 8, 74–78.

Fox, L.H. (1979) Programs for the gifted and talented: an overview. In: Passow, A.H. (Ed) *The Gifted and Talented: Their Education and Development*. University of Chicago Press.

Frampton, O. (nd) *Slow learners, segregated and integrated*. Research report, Education Department, University of Christchurch, New Zealand.

*Galton, M., Simon, B. & Croll, P. (1980) *Inside the Primary Classroom*. Routledge.

Gamoran, A. (1987) Organization, instruction and the effects of ability grouping: comments on Slavin's 'Best–Evidence Synthesis'. *Review of Educational Research,* 57(3), 341–345.

Gamoran, A. & Berends, M. (1987) The effects of stratification in secondary schools: synthesis of survey and ethnographic research. *Review of Educational Research,* 57 (4) 415–435.

Gamoran, A., Nystand, M., Berends, M. & LePore, P. (1995) An organisational analysis of the effects of ability grouping. *American Educational Research Journal,* 32 (4), 687–715.

Gewitz, S., Ball, S. & Bowe, R. (1993) Values and ethics in the education market place: the case of Northwark Park. *International Studies in Sociology of Education,* 3, 233–254.

Glass, G., McGaw, B. & Smith, M.L. (1981) *Meta–analysis in Social Research.* Beverly Hills, CA: Sage.

Goldberg, M.L., Passow, A.H. & Justman, J. (1966) *The Effects of Ability Groupings.* New York: Teachers' College Press.

Goldstein, H. & Noss, R. (1990) Against the stream. *Forum* 3 (1), 4–6.

*Good, T.L. & Marshall, S. (1984) Do students learn more in heterogeneous or homogeneous groups? In: Peterson, P., Wilkinson, L. Cherry & Hallinan, M. (Eds) *Student Diversity and the Organization, Process and Use of Instructional Groups in the Classroom.* New York: Academic Press.

*Gregory, R.P. (1984) Streaming, setting and mixed ability grouping in primary and secondary schools: some research findings. *Educational Studies,* 10 (3).

Hacker, R.G., Rowe, M.J. & Evans, R.D. (1991) The influences of ability groupings for secondary science lessons upon classroom processes. *School Science Review,* 73 (262), 125.

Hacker, R. G., Rowe, M.J. & Evans, R.D. (1992) The influences of ability groupings for secondary science lessons upon classroom processes. Part 2. *School Science Review,* 73 (264), 119–123.

Hallam, S. & Toutounji, I. (1996) *What do we Know about the Grouping of Pupils by Ability? A research review.* London University Institute of Education.

Hargreaves, D. (1967) *Social Relations in a Secondary School.* Routledge and Kegan Paul.

Harrah, D.D. (1956) A study of the effectiveness of five kinds of grouping in the classroom. *Dissertation Abstracts International,* 17, 715 (University Microfilms No 56–1114).

Hart, R.H. (1962) The nongraded primary school and arithmetic. *The Arithmetic Teacher,* 9, 130–133.

Hartill, R. (1936) *Homogeneous Groupings as a Policy in the Elementary Schools in New York City.* Contributions to Education No 690. New York: Teachers' College, Columbia.

HMI (1978) *Mixed Ability Work in Comprehensive Schools.* Matters for Discussion Series 6. HMSO.

Hoffer, T.B. (1992) Middle school ability grouping and student achievement in science and mathematics. *Educational Evaluation and Policy Analysis,* 14 (3), 205–227.

Ingram, V. (1960) Flint evaluates its primary cycle. *Elementary School Journal,* 61, 76–80.

Jackson, B. (1964) *Streaming: An Education System in Miniature.* Routledge and Kegan Paul.

Jones, D.M. (1948) An experiment in adaption to individual differences. *Journal of Educational Psychology,* 39, 257–273.

Justman, J. (1968) Reading and Class Homogeneity. *Reading Teacher,* 21, 314–316.

Kelly, A.V. (1975) *Case Studies in Mixed Ability Teaching.* Harper & Row.

Kerchkoff, A.C. (1986) Effects of ability grouping in British secondary schools. *American Sociological Review,* 51 (6), 842–858.

Kerry, T. (1982a) Mixed ability teaching in the humanities. In: Sands, M. & Kerry, T. (Eds) *Mixed Ability Teaching.* Croom Helm.

Kerry, T. (1982b) The demands made on pupils' thinking in mixed ability classes. In: Sands, M. & Kerry, T. (Eds) *Mixed Ability Teaching.* Croom Helm.

Koontz, W.F. (1961) A study of achievement as a function of homogeneous grouping. *Journal of Experimental Education,* 30, 249–253.

Kulik, C. & Kulik, J. (1984) Effects of accelerated instruction on students. *Review of Educational Research,* 54, 409–425.

Lacey, C. (1970) *Hightown Grammar: the School as a Social System.* Manchester University Press.

*Lee, J. & Croll, P. (1995) Streaming and subject specialism at Key Stage 2: survey in two local authorities. *Educational Studies,* 21, 2.

Leiter, J. (1983) Classroom composition and achievement gains. *Sociology of Education,* 56, 126–132.

Linchevski, L. (1995a) 'Tell me who your classmates are and I'll tell you what you are learning: mixed ability versus ability grouping in mathematics classes'. Paper presented at MES seminar held at King's College, London.

Linchevski, L. (1995b) *Tell me who your classmates are and I'll tell you what you learn.* PME XIX, 3, 240–247. Recife, Brazil.

Loomer, B.M. (1962) Ability grouping and its effects upon individual achievement. *Dissertation Abstracts,* 232, 1581 (University Microfilms No 62–4982).

Lou, Y., Abrami, P.C., Spence, J.C., Poulsen, C., Chambers, B. & d'Apollonia, S. (1996) Within-class grouping: a meta-analysis. *Review of Educational Research,* 66 (4) 423–458.

*McNamara, D.R. & Waugh, D.G. (1993) Classroom organisation: a discussion of grouping strategies in the light of the 'Three Wise Men's' report. *School Organisation,* 13 (1).

McPake, J., Harlen, W., Powney, J. & Davidson, J. (1999) *Teachers' and Pupils' Days in the Primary Classroom.* Edinburgh: SCRE.

McPhee, A. (1978) *Mixed Ability and Streamed Groupings in Third Year Secondary English.* Edinburgh: Scottish Curriculum Development Service.

Marascuilo, L.A. & McSweeney, M. (1972) Tracking and minority student attitudes and performance. *Urban Education,* 6, 303–319.

Martin, W.H. (1927) The results of homogeneous grouping in the junior high school. Unpublished doctoral dissertation, Yale University.

*Mason, D.A. (1995) Grouping students for elementary school mathematics: a survey of principals in 12 states. *Educational Research and Evaluation,* 1 (4), 318–346.

Medwell, J. *et al* (1998) *Effective Teachers of Literacy: A Report of a Research Project Commissioned by the Teacher Training Agency.* University of Exeter School of Education.

Mikkelson, J.E. (1962) 'An experimental study of selective grouping and acceleration in junior high school mathematics'. Unpublished doctoral dissertation, University of Minnesota.

Morgenstern, A. (1963) A comparison of the effects of heterogeneous (ability) groupings on the academic achievement and personal–social adjustment of sixth grade children. *Dissertation Abstracts,* 23, 1054 (University Microfilms No 63–6560).

Morrice, J. (1999) Calculated move. *Times Educational Supplement Scotland,* March 19.

Morris, V.P. (1969) An evaluation of pupil achievement in a nongraded primary plan after three, and also five years of instruction. *Dissertation Abstracts,* 29, 3809–A (University Microfilms No 63–6560).

Morrison, C. (1976) *Ability Grouping and Mixed Ability Grouping in Secondary Schools.* Edinburgh: Scottish Council for Research in Education.

*Mortimore, P., Sammons, P., Stoll, L., Lewis, D. & Ecob, R. (1988) *School Matters: The Junior Years.* Wells: Open Books.

Moses, P.J. (1966) A study of inter–class ability grouping on achievement in reading. *Dissertation Abstracts,* 26, 4342.

Neave, G. (1975) *How They Fared: The Impact of the Comprehensive School on the University*. Henley: Routledge and Kegan Paul.

Newbold, D. (1977) *Ability Grouping – the Banbury Enquiry*. Slough: NFER.

Oakes, J. (1995) Two cities' tracking and within–school segregation. *Teachers' College Record*, 96 (4).

Oakes, J., Gamoran, A. & Page, R.N. (1992) Curriculum differentiation: opportunities, outcomes, and meanings. In: Jackson, P.W. (Ed) *Handbook of Research on Curriculum*. Washington DC: American Educational Research Association.

OfSTED (Office for Standards in Education) (1993) *Curriculum Organisation and Classroom Practice in Primary Schools: a follow–up report*. Department for Education.

OfSTED (Office for Standards in Education) (1998) *Standards and Quality in Education 1996/7. The Annual Report of Her Majesty's Chief Inspector of Schools*. HMSO.

Peterson, R.L. (1966) 'An experimental study of the effects of ability grouping in grades 7 and 8'. Unpublished doctoral dissertation, University of Minnesota.

*Plewes, J.A. (1979) Mixed ability teaching: a deterioration in performance. *Journal of Research in Science Teaching*, 16, 229–236.

Postlethwaite, K. & Denton, C. (1978) *Streams for the future: the long term effects of early streaming and non–streaming. The final report of the Banbury Enquiry*. Banbury: Pubansco Publications.

Prais, S.J. (1997) Whole-class teaching, school-readiness and pupils' mathematical attainments. *Oxford Review of Education*, 23 (3), 275 -290.

Provus, M.M. (1960) Ability grouping in arithmetic. *Elementary School Journal*, 60, 391–398.

Rankin, P.T., Anderson, C.T. & Bergman, W.G. (1936) Ability Grouping in the Detroit Individualisation Experiment. In: While, G.M. (Ed) *The Grading of Pupils: Thirty–fifth Year Book of the National Society for the Study of Education (Part 1)*. Bloomington, Ill: Public School Publishing Co.

*Reid, M., Clunies–Ross, L., Goacher, B. & Vile, C. (1981) Mixed ability teaching: problems and possibilities. Accessed through a summary by David Upton, *Educational Research*, 24 (1).

Rosenbaum, J. (1976) *Making Inequality: The Hidden Curriculum of High School Tracking*. New York: Wiley.

Ross, J., Bunton, W.J., Evison, P. & Robertson, T.S. (1972) *A Critical Appraisal of Comprehensive Schooling: A Research Report*. Slough: NFER.

Ross, J.M. & Simpson, H.R. (1971) The national survey of health and development 2: Rate of school progress between 8 and 15 years and between 15 and 18 years. *British Journal of Educational Psychology*, 4, 125–135.

Rudd, W.G.A. (1956) Psychological effects of streaming with special reference to a group of selected children. *British Journal of Educational Psychology*, 28, 47–60.

Schwartz, F. (1981) Supporting or subverting learning: peer group patterns in four tracked schools. *Anthropology and Education Quarterly*, 12, 99–121.

Simpson, M. (1997) Developing differentiation practices: meeting the needs of pupils and teachers. *The Curriculum Journal*, 8 (1) 85–104.

Simpson, M., Cameron, P., Goulder, J., Duncan, A., Roberts, A. & Smithers, I. (1989) *Differentiation in the primary School: Investigations of Learning and Teaching*. Aberdeen: Northern College.

Simpson, M. & Ure, J. (1993) *What's the Difference? A Study of Differentiation in Scottish Secondary Schools*. Aberdeen: Northern College.

Skapski, M.K. (1960) Ungraded primary reading program: an objective evaluation. *The Elementary School Journal*, 61, 41–45.

Slavin, R.E. (1984) Meta–analysis in education: how is it being used? *Educational Researcher*, 13 (8), 6–15 and 24–27.

*Slavin, R.E. (1986) Best-evidence synthesis: an alternative to meta-analytic and traditional reviews. *Educational Researcher*, November 1986, 5–11.

*Slavin, R.E. (1987) Ability grouping and student achievement in elementary schools: a best–evidence synthesis. *Review of Educational Research*, 57 (3), 293–336.

*Slavin, R.E. (1990) Student achievement effects of ability grouping in secondary schools: a best–evidence synthesis. *Review of Educational Research*, 60 (3), 471–499.

Slavin, R.E. (1993) Ability grouping in middle grades: Achievement effects and alternatives. *Elementary School Journal*, 93 (5) 535–552.

Slavin, R.E. & Karweit, N.L. (1985) Effects of whole class, ability grouped, and individualized instruction on mathematics achievement. *American Educational Research Journal*, 22, 351–367.

Smith, L. (1986) From psychology to instruction. In: Harris, J. (Ed) *Child Psychology in Action: Linking Research and Practice*. Croom Helm.

Smith, W.M. (1960) The effect of intra–class ability grouping on arithmetic achievement in grades 2 through 5. *Dissertation Abstracts International*, 21, 563–564.

SOEID (Scottish Office Education and Industry Department) (1996) *Achievement for All: A Report on Selection Within Schools by HM Inspectors of Schools.* Edinburgh: Scottish Office Education and Industry Department.

SOEID (Scottish Office Education and Industry Department) (1999) *Standards and Quality in Scottish Schools, 1995–98.* Edinburgh: Scottish Office Education and Industry Department.

Spear, R.C. (1994) Teacher perceptions of ability grouping practices in middle level schools. *Research in Middle Level Education*, 18 (1) 117–139.

Spence, E.S. (1958) Intra–class grouping of pupils for instruction in arithmetic in the intermediate grades of the elementary school. *Dissertation Abstracts International,* 19, 1682 (University Microfilms No 58–5635).

Stern, A.M. (1972) Intra–class grouping of low achievers in mathematics in the third and fourth grades. *Dissertation Abstracts International,* 32, 5539–A (University Microfilms No 73–11900).

Sukhnandan, L. with Lee, B. (1998) *Streaming, Setting and Grouping by Ability: a Review of the Literature.* Slough: NFER.

Svenson, N.E. (1965) *Ability grouping and scholastic achievement.* Studies in Educational Psychology, No 5. Stockholm: Almquist and Wiksell.

*Taylor, N. (1993) Ability grouping and its effect on pupil behaviour: a case study of a Midlands comprehensive school. *Education Today*, 43 (2).

Thomas, R.M. (1987) The individual and the group. In: Dunkin, M.J. (Ed) *The International Encyclopaedia of Teaching and Teacher Education.* Oxford: Pergamon Press.

Thompson, D. (1974) Non–streaming did make a difference? *Forum for the Discussion of New Trends in Education*, 16 (2).

Tobin, J.F. (1966) 'An eight–year study of classes grouped within grade levels on the basis of reading ability'. Doctoral dissertation, Boston University (University Microfilms No 66–345).

Tomlinson, S. (1987) Curriculum option choices in multi-ethnic schools. In: Troyna, B. (Ed) *Racial Inequality in Education.* London: Tavistock.

Torgelson, J.W. (1963) 'A comparison of homogeneous and heterogeneous grouping for below average junior high school students'. Unpublished doctoral dissertation, University of Minnesota.

Troyna, B. (1991) Underachievers or underrated? The experience of pupils of South Asian Origin in a secondary school. *British Educational Research Journal*, 17 (4) 361–376.

Tuckman, B.W. & Bierman, M. (1971) *Beyond Pygmalion: Galatea in the Schools.* Arlington, Virginia: Computer Microfilm International Corporation.

Valentine, J., Clart, D.D., Irvin, J.L., Kefe, J.W. & Melton, G. (1993) *Leadership in Middle Level Education: A National Survey of Middle Level Leaders and Schools* (Vol 1) Reston, Virginia: National Association of Secondary School Principals.

*Wallen, N.E. & Vowles, R.O. (1960) The effects of inter–class ability grouping on arithmetic achievement in the sixth grade. *Journal of Educational Psychology,* 51, 159–163.

*Watson, K. (1985) Mixed-ability classrooms produce superior results. *Highway One,* Fall 1985, 57.

Webb, N. (1982) 'Predicting learning from student interaction: defining the variables'. Paper presented at the Annual Meeting of the American Educational Research Association, New York City.

Weinstein, R. (1976) Reading group membership in first grade: teacher behaviours and pupil experience over time. *Journal of Educational Psychology,* 68, 103–116.

Whitehead, F., Capey, A.C., Maddren, W. & Wellings, A. (1977) *Children and Their Books.* Macmillan Education.

Wilcox, J. (1961) 'A search for multiple effects of grouping upon growth and behaviour of junior high school pupils'. Dissertation, Cornell University.

Wilkinson, L.C. (1988–9) Grouping children for learning: implications for kindergarten education. In: Rothkopf, E.Z. (Ed) *Review of Research and Education,* 15, 203–223.

Winn, W & Wilson, A.P. (1983) The affect and effect of ability grouping. *Contemporary Education,* 54, 119–125.

*Wragg, E.C. (1984) (Ed) *Classroom Teaching Skills: the Research Findings of the Teacher Education Project.* Routledge.